The Fourth Beast

Monroe Sinclair

ISBN: 978-1-4421-7527-3

Table of Contents

Appendix I

INTRODUCTION

Ultimately, all Bible prophecy climaxes at the showdown between two kings: Jesus Christ and Satan. To add anything more to this prophetic inevitability would detract from its simplicity: good versus evil, heaven versus hell, God versus Satan, life versus death. This showdown is prophesied to take place along the valley of Jezreel near Mount Megiddo. It is from the word Meggido that the word "Armageddon" is derived. Today, the word Armageddon is as much a part of the doomsday lexicon as the number "666."

Of course, for all the interest and mystique the War of Armageddon generates, the event itself is prophesied to be a swift, decisive outcome with Christ obliterating His ancient adversary, not to mention the multi-million man army that will accompany him. For all of the hype associated with it, Armageddon will one day go down in history as the most lopsided war the world will ever witness.

While the date of this titanic clash remains shrouded in mystery, the interest surrounding it and speculation concerning the events leading up to it remain a source of great debate. While there are many different interpretations or models of eschatology that attempt to decipher how the events leading up to Armageddon will unfold, the Bible offers a very peculiar model involving beasts.

This prophetic "beast" model that I propose is unique to anything I have ever read. I believe that a particular series of events leading up to Armageddon can be understood once specific interpretations are applied to these beasts. The interpretations offer specific insight into, not only things which have come to pass, but things which shall come to pass. That which shall come to pass can only be derived or understood from what has already been:

> The thing that hath been, it is that which shall be; and that which is done is that which shall be done: and there is no new thing under the sun. (Ecclesiastes 1:9)

Traditional prophetic models have defined the four beasts of Daniel 7:4–7 as representing the same four kingdoms outlined in the great image of Daniel 2. Using this prophetic model, a vast number of pre-millennial scholars believe these four beasts represent the kingdoms of Babylon, Medo-Persia, Greece, and Rome, respectively.

If this successive kingdom theory held true, the four kingdoms outlined in Daniel 2 would simply be repeated in Daniel 7. On the face of it, this would appear highly suspicious, especially considering the drastically different imagery employed within the two chapters, along with the fact each vision was given at two separate points in time. While the great image of Daniel 2 is the image of a man, the four beasts of Daniel 7 are images of monstrous creatures from the sea. This raises the question of whether or not the four kingdoms of Babylon, Medo-Persia, Greece, and Rome outlined in the great image are perfectly represented in the four beasts of Daniel 7.

In my opinion, a very innocent oversight occurs in Daniel 7:23.

> Thus he said, the fourth beast shall be the fourth kingdom upon earth, which shall be diverse from all kingdoms, and shall devour the whole earth, and shall tread it down, and break it in pieces. (Daniel 7:23)

Logic would seem to demonstrate that, since the fourth beast of Daniel 7:7 defines the fourth kingdom, the three beasts before him must define kingdoms as well. However, a problem arises when Daniel 7:17 expressly defines these four beasts as four kings:

> These great beasts, which are four, are four kings, which shall arise out of the earth. (Daniel 7:17)

A considerable number of pre-millennial scholars have uniformly replaced the "kings" with "kingdoms," and therefore drawn a direct parallel between the four kingdoms outlined in Daniel 2 and the four beasts in Daniel 7. However, there is a distinct difference between a king and a kingdom. While a kingdom defines the dominion of a king, a king himself can be defined as a man. Furthermore, the duration of a kingdom is virtually unlimited in its scope, ranging anywhere from hundreds of years to as little as one day, while the duration of a king is much more limited, as it cannot extend beyond the number of years a king or queen is actually alive.

If someone were to apply a literal interpretation to the fourth beast in Daniel 7, it could be said this beast represents both a king (Daniel 7:17) and a kingdom (Daniel 7:23). Now this is a very unusual interpretation to say the least, as the Bible usually makes a distinction between a king and a kingdom. However, while this interpretation may appear illogical, it is not unconditional.

> After this I saw in the night visions, and behold a fourth beast, dreadful and terrible, and strong exceedingly; and it had great iron teeth: it devoured and brake in pieces, and stamped the residue with the feet of it: *and it was diverse from all the beasts that there were before it*; and it had ten horns. (Daniel 7:7) [italics mine]

The fourth beast is specifically related as being "diverse from all the beasts that were before it." In addition to representing a king and kingdom, this fourth beast is being further defined as "diverse." In other words, not only does this fourth beast represent both a king and kingdom, but it specifically represents a diverse king and a diverse kingdom.

The questions that must be reconciled not only include how to fulfill a prophecy that calls for a fourth beast to represent a king and kingdom, but additionally how this diversity applies to a king and kingdom.

Also, note how this dilemma is further compounded by the lack of detail offered the fourth beast. While the descriptions offered the first three beasts in Daniel 7:4–6 appear fully fleshed out to the last detail, the fourth great beast is given very little. Why is this? If the fourth great beast represents both a diverse king and kingdom, it would seem that even more description would be necessary to gain insight into who or what this beast is. It is a very curious omission to say the least.

Oddly enough, Daniel literally witnesses the destruction of the "body" of the fourth beast.

> I beheld then because of the voice of the great words which the horn spake: *I beheld even till the beast was slain, and his body destroyed,* and given to the burning flame. (Daniel 7:11) [italics mine]

While Daniel does indeed witness bodily destruction of this fourth beast, he never describes it in detail anywhere within the chapter. Instead of a detailed bodily account, like the beasts in Daniel 7:4-6, the descriptions of the fourth beast are scattered and hazy ("great iron teeth" [7:7], "ten horns" [7:7], "nails of brass" [7:19], and a "head" [7:20]).

My contention is simple, if Daniel saw the body of the fourth beast destroyed, yet never describes it, then it stands to reason its body must be related elsewhere in the Bible.

This naturally brings us to text of Revelation 13:1–2, where a beast similar to the one related in Daniel 7:7 rises up out of the the sea.

> And I stood upon the sand of the sea, and saw a beast rise up out of the sea, having seven heads and ten horns, and upon his horns ten crowns, and upon his heads the name of blasphemy. And the beast which I saw was like unto a leopard, and his feet were as the feet of a bear, and his mouth as the mouth of a lion: and the dragon gave him his power, and his seat, and great authority. (Revelation 13:1–2)

Note how the body of the beast in Revelation 13:1-2 (leopard, bear, and lion) perfectly aligns with the three beasts outlined in Daniel 7:4–6. It appears as if an undeniable connection exists between the beast of Revelation 13 and the fourth beast of Daniel 7. But what exactly is this connection? Is it related to chronology, identity, or location? Perhaps it relates to all three of them.

If the fourth beast of Daniel 7:7 is the final beast that "rises out of the sea" in both the books of Daniel and Revelation, the fact the book of Daniel was written more than 600 years before the book of Revelation would have offered God an interesting opportunity to provide Daniel a glimpse of the final beast to come. And in doing so, impart critical information that might allow us to understand exactly who, what, where, and when this final beast is. In short, the vague body of the fourth beast in Daniel 7 could be asking us to build it for ourselves.

In order to understand the body of the fourth beast in Daniel 7, one must first examine the three beasts that came before it. Who exactly are these three beasts? How do these beasts relate to the beasts outlined in the book of Revelation? Who are the beasts of Revelation? When do they rise to power? Where are they?

When these questions are answered, a specific pattern begins to emerge. This pattern not only explains what this fourth beast is, but it also explains why the Daniel was told to close up and seal the words of this book until the time of the end. I am convinced this "time of the end" really ended around 95 A.D., when John of Patmos finished writing the book of Revelation. The Roman Age that was concealed in the book of Daniel is revealed in the book of Revelation. Likewise, the non-Roman era that was concealed in the book of Revelation is revealed in the book of Daniel. It appears that the books of Daniel and Revelation unseal each other. If this is true, then the body of the fourth beast that Daniel saw destroyed in Daniel 7:11 must be fully revealed in the book of Revelation.

CHAPTER 1:

THE FOUR GREAT BEASTS

In the first year of King Belshazzar's reign as king of Babylon in 549 B.C., Daniel began to dream and have visions while he slept. In Daniel 7:1 we read that, upon waking, "he wrote the dream, and told the sum of the matters."

Because the "sum of the matters" concerned the dreams Daniel was having, this "one" that "stood by and made known the interpretation" (Daniel 7:16) is never described, though it's likely Daniel was speaking with an angel.

> These great beasts, which are four, are four kings which shall arise out of the earth. (Daniel 7:17)

There is little room for error here. Daniel 7:17 expressly defines these four great beasts as four kings or rulers of men: individual men who will rise to the authority of kings of the earth.

Four Beasts of Daniel 7
Represent four individual kings

While the "sea" in which the beasts rise up from is never defined, most Bible prophecy experts believe it represents the Gentile kingdoms of men. The problem with this interpretation, though, is that it contradicts the interpretation offered in Daniel 7:17.

> These great beasts, which are four, are four kings, which shall arise out of the earth. (Daniel 7:17)

Daniel 7:17 makes it clear how the four beasts represent four individual kings, not kingdoms. While many pre-millennial scholars believe that the word "kings" can be substituted for the word "kingdoms", Daniel 7:17 makes it clear that it cannot. It appears that the reason for doing this stems from a desire to perfectly harmonize the "four kingdoms" related in Daniel 2 with the "four beasts" related in Daniel 7. If the four beasts do indeed represent "kingdoms" instead of "kings," then this would present a perfect model from which to operate. According to many pre-millennial scholars, the four kingdoms outlined in Daniel 2 represent the kingdoms of Babylon, Medo-Persia, Greece, and Rome. They also believe these kingdoms represent the four beasts in Daniel 7:4–7.

The problem with this interpretation is that it conflicts with the interpretation offered in Daniel 7:17. In the following section, I will examine the question of whether or not the first three beasts related in Daniel 7:4-6 should be understood in terms of "kingdoms" or "kings".

BEAST 1:

KING NEBUCHADNEZZAR
(605 B.C. – 562 B.C.)

> The first was like a lion, and had eagle's wings: I beheld till the wings thereof were plucked, and it was lifted up from the earth, and made to stand upon the feet as a man, and a man's heart was given to it. (Daniel 7:4)

The key to understanding if this passage is speaking of a king or kingdom is to employ a method of literal interpretation. Note how this beast is described as being "lifted up from the earth, and made to stand upon the feet as a "man and a man's heart was given to it."

This raises the question, can a man's heart be given to a kingdom?

The answer is an emphatic, no.

Furthermore, how can a kingdom can be described as standing upon its feet as a man? Let alone the Babylonian Empire, a kingdom that was destroyed because of its wickedness. The symbolic meaning behind the "man's heart" being given this first beast clearly applies to King Nebuchadnezzar, and the salvation-type experience he underwent after he acknowledged the God of heaven as the sole grantor of his dominion in Daniel 4:34. And while this symbolic redemption could never be applied to the Babylonian Empire, it can easily apply to a Babylonian king.

Daniel 4 and 5 is the compelling story of Nebuchadnezzar's sudden fall from kingship and ultimate redemption is detailed. Daniel 5:20 states that Nebuchadnezzar's great fall came about as a result of his erroneously prideful conviction that the power of his empire was rooted in his own strength as its king. According to Daniel 4:33, this faulty declaration uttered in Daniel 4:30 brought the judgment of God.

However, the passages in Daniel 4:34–37 relate that at the end of Nebuchadnezzar's seven year exile from the throne, he finally acknowledged the God of Abraham, Isaac, and Jacob as sole proprietor of his power. As a result, he was restored to the throne of Babylon.

After this restoration, God rewarded Nebuchadnezzar with a kingdom much greater than the one he possessed before. Thus, when we read in Daniel 7:4 that his "wings thereof were plucked, and it was lifted up from the earth, and made to stand upon the feet as a man, and a man's heart was given to it," this symbolizes the prideful rise and fall of Nebuchadnezzar before he finally acknowledged the God of Abraham. After acknowledging the God of Abraham, God restored him to his throne, providing him with a much greater dominion than the one he had previously possessed.

BEAST 2:

CYRUS THE GREAT
(539 B.C. – 529 B.C.)

And behold another beast, a second, like to a bear, and it raised up itself on one side, and it had three ribs in the mouth of it, between the teeth of it: and they said thus unto it, Arise, devour much flesh. (Daniel 7:5)

Cyrus the Great officially succeeded Darius the Mede as king of the Medo-Persian Empire in 536 B.C. However, in 539 B.C., it was Cyrus who led his vastly superior Persian army into Babylon on the fateful night God pronounced judgment upon the Babylonian Empire. While it is true that Cyrus the Great first took the Persian throne sometime in the 550's B.C., it was not until he joined forces with Darius and the Medes in 539 B.C. that their empires were forged into a single, unified power.

Because the Persian Empire was so much stronger than the Median Empire, the beast of Daniel 7:5 is described as being "raised up on one side." This lopsidedness represents the superior strength of the Persian Empire.

The three ribs in the bear's mouth represent the three major conquests the Medo-Persian Empire sustained under Cyrus. Together with the

Medes, Cyrus and his army captured Babylon to the west, Assyria to the south, and Palestine to the east.

The command, "Arise, devour much flesh" prophetically foreshadows the mighty vastness of Cyrus's kingdom. Throughout his reign as king, and up until the time of his death in 529 B.C., Cyrus amassed an empire that stretched as far east as the border of India and as far west as the Mediterranean Sea. The northern boundary reached the foot of the Caucasus Mountains of southern Russia, while the southern boundary stretched as far south as Egypt.

It was by all accounts a magnificent empire, and it flourished for many generations after Cyrus's death. And it most certainly would have lasted for many more if it weren't for a young, brash Macedonian king from the West.

BEAST 3:

ALEXANDER THE GREAT
(336 B.C. – 323 B.C.)

After this I beheld, and lo another, like a leopard, which had upon the back of it four wings of a fowl; the beast had also four heads; and dominion was given to it. (Daniel 7:6)

No king before or since has conquered the world with such a rapid explosion of force. History books are littered with this legend's brilliantly conceived conquests. Beginning in 336 B.C., Alexander conquered most all the known world in five short years. The leopard symbolically represents the amazing swiftness of Alexander's conquests.

The "four wings of a fowl" represent the vast expansion of Alexander's kingdom from all four directions: north, south, east, and west.

After Alexander's death in 323 B.C., his kingdom was split among his four generals: Cassander, Lysimachus, Ptolemy, and Seleucus. Thus, the four heads of the beast represent these four generals.

Alexander's kingdom endured until around 30 B.C. Many of the programs and policies he instituted during his brief but fruitful reign are still around today. Much has been written and conjectured about this great king. In fact, many would argue that Alexander's influence upon the western world was perhaps greater than that of any Gentile king who ever lived.

But this distinction will not be held for long. The Bible relates the story of another king. A mighty king whose power and influence will one day not only eclipse those of his predecessors, but utterly lay waste the notion of influence and boundary altogether. This man's kingdom will extend into the far reaches of the most remote wilderness and his power will influence all those who dwell upon the earth. His influence will not only be felt, but *demanded* upon all those who witness his reign (Revelation 13:8). It is clear that this man seeks more than a passing allegiance to each of those who occupy his world-wide empire. He will require complete and total worship. Perhaps, most frightening of all, he will receive it.

THE FOURTH GREAT BEAST

A KING AND KINGDOM
(? A.D. – ? A.D.)

> After this I saw in the night visions, and behold a fourth beast, dreadful and terrible, and strong exceedingly; and it had great iron teeth: it devoured and brake in pieces and stamped the residue with the feet of it: and it from all the beasts that were before it; and it had ten horns. (Daniel 7:7)

Like the three great beasts before him, this fourth great beast is a "king" (Daniel 7:17). However, in Daniel 7:23, we also read where this beast represents a "kingdom":

Thus he said, the fourth beast shall be the fourth kingdom upon earth, which shall be diverse from all kingdoms, and shall devour the whole earth, and shall tread it down, and brake it in pieces. (Daniel 7:7)

Unlike the three great beasts before him, who only related individual kings, this fourth great beast represents both a king and a kingdom.

So what exactly are the texts of Daniel 7:17 and Daniel 7:23 attempting to explain about the unique beast of Daniel 7:7? Is it relating that this individual man ("king") in some way is an empire ("kingdom") unto himself? Or is it the other way around?

For a moment, let's explore the possibilities. Could this be a conditional prophecy? One in which either the king or kingdom could come to pass before the other? In other words, could this prophecy involve a situation where a *king* arises, but until he establishes his *kingdom*, the prophecy of Daniel 7:7 cannot be fulfilled? Or the kingdom will come to pass, but until the actual *king* arises, the prophecy cannot be fulfilled? There are myriad questions that arise.

But first let's deal with what we do know. If we look back in Daniel 2, we are presented an image of this fourth kingdom.

And the fourth kingdom shall be strong as iron: forasmuch as iron breaketh in pieces and subdueth all things: and as iron breaketh all these: shall it break in pieces and bruise. And whereas thou sawest the feet and toes, part of potters' clay, and part of iron, the kingdom shall be divided; but there shall be in it the strength of the iron, forasmuch as thou sawest the iron mixed with miry clay. And as the toes of the feet were part of iron, and part of clay, so the kingdom shall be partly strong and partly broken. (Daniel 2:40–42)

Most biblical scholars agree that the "legs of iron" on the great image represent the Roman Empire. Since the "iron" aspect of the Roman Empire is represented in both the "legs of iron" and the kingdom that succeeds it in the "feet and toes of iron and clay," many believe this kingdom of "feet and toes of iron and clay" represents the modern manifestation of the old Roman Empire, which today is recognized as the European Union.

The reason the European Union is recognized by many pre-millennial scholars as the modern manifestation of the Roman Empire is the result of a "Treaty of Rome" that was established in 1957. This treaty forged an alliance between the countries of Belgium, West Germany, France, Luxembourg, Netherlands, and Italy. This was the first time since the glory days of the Old Roman Empire that European countries were aligned together under a common treaty.

While the four kingdoms of Babylon, Medo-Persia, Greece, and Rome present a very clear model of four successive kingdoms, it should be noted that this great image in Daniel 2 is actually comprised of five unique elements: head of gold, chest and arms of silver, belly and thighs of brass, legs of iron, and feet and toes of iron and clay.

Five Elements presented in Daniel 2:
1. Head of Gold (Babylonian Empire)
2. Chest and Arms of Silver (Medo-Persian Empire)
3. Belly and Thighs of Brass (Greek Empire)
4. Legs of Iron (Fourth Kingdom here?)
5. Feet and Toes of Iron and Clay (Or here?)

A SUSPICIOUS LACK OF CLARITY

One of the more curious aspects of Daniel's interpretation regarding the great image in Daniel 2 is the lack of any clear distinction between the kingdoms represented in the "legs of iron" and "feet and toes of iron and clay."

While it is clear the kingdom represented in the "legs of iron" is the Roman Empire, the essential question is not whether the Roman Empire is represented, but whether or not it precisely fulfills the conditions regarding the fourth kingdom outlined in Daniel 2:40–41 and Daniel 7:23. If the Roman Empire does not represent these conditions, but instead is exclusively represented in "legs of iron," then what exactly is this kingdom represented in the "feet and toes or iron and clay" relating?

Central dilemma regarding image of Daniel 2
Is the Roman Empire the fourth kingdom?

While most pre-millennial scholars will argue how this lack of clarity stems from the fact the fourth kingdom represents both the "legs of iron" (Roman Empire) and the "feet and toes of iron and clay" (the European Union), I would argue that while the European Union certainly might fulfill the role required of the fourth kingdom, it is impossible the European Union alone fulfills the requirement. The reason for this is rather simple. The European Union alone cannot represent the fourth kingdom because the fourth kingdom is defined within the context of the fourth beast. And since the fourth beast is defined within the context of both a human "king" (Dan. 7:17) and a "kingdom" (Dan. 7:23), the fourth kingdom must be defined within the context of an individual king as well.

Put very simply, the beast of Daniel 7:7 represents both a "king" and a "kingdom" *at the same time.* By virtue of this fact, it stands to reason the European Union alone cannot represent the fourth kingdom. Therefore, the fundamental question that arises is, how can the fourth beast be defined within the context of both a king and kingdom at the same time?

Since the chronological possibility exists that either the fourth king or fourth kingdom could arise before the other, if one presumes the European Union is this fourth kingdom, then until the fourth king comes along to establish it, the European Union cannot definitively represent the fourth kingdom.

Fortunately, the text of Daniel 7:7 takes this king and kingdom interpretation one step further. Note how the adjective "diverse" is applied to describe this fourth beast.

Fourth Beast of Daniel 7:7
Is "Diverse"

Once this "diversity" is understood and applied to both a king and kingdom, only then can we precisely establish what this fourth beast represents.

DANIEL'S EMPIRE SKIP

While it is definitely true that we cannot precisely determine what this fourth beast represents until the term "diverse" can be understood, we are shown something extraordinary in Daniel 7:25:

> Thus he said, the fourth beast shall be the fourth kingdom upon earth, which shall be diverse from all kingdoms, and shall devour the whole earth, and shall tread it down, and break it in pieces. And the ten horns out of this kingdom are ten kings that shall arise: and another shall rise after them; and he shall be diverse from the first, and shall subdue three kings. And he shall speak great words against the most High, and shall wear out the saints of the most High, and think to change times and laws: and they shall be given into his hand *until a time and times and the dividing time*. (Daniel 7:23-25) [italics mine]

According to the final passage in Daniel 7:25, the duration of the fourth kingdom will be one that specifically encompasses three and one-half years ("a time and times and the dividing time"). By virtue of the fact this fourth kingdom can only endure for three and one-half years, we can understand how this fourth kingdom cannot represent the Roman Empire represented in the "legs of iron". After all, the historical Roman Empire endured for nearly one thousand five-hundred years.

In fact, since Daniel 7:27 relates how the kingdom that immediately succeeds the fourth kingdom "shall be given to the people of the saints of the most High and is an everlasting kingdom," the only kingdom in which this fourth one can correspond is the fifth element presented in the image's "feet and toes of iron and clay" from Daniel 2.

Fourth Kingdom in Daniel 7:23
Exclusively represents the Feet and Toes of Iron and Clay

If the fourth kingdom represents the "feet and toes of iron and clay," then what happened to the Roman Empire represented in the "legs of iron"? Why doesn't the fourth element represented in the "legs of iron" correspond to the fourth kingdom? Furthermore, why isn't the kingdom that represents the "feet and toes of iron and clay" called the fifth kingdom, since this really is what it is?

One rather weak argument that Bible scholars use to support the idea that both the kingdoms represented in the "legs of iron" and "feet and toes of iron and clay" are Roman is the fact the fourth beast that possesses "teeth of iron" (Dan. 7:7). If both the kingdoms represented in the "legs of iron" and beast with "teeth of iron" contain the iron element, then how could they not represent the same thing? This contention, though, falls flat in light of the fact the fourth beast also possesses "nails of brass" (Daniel 7:19). Using this logic, anyone who claims the fourth kingdom represents a Greek Empire instead of a Roman one would have just as valid an argument.

Personally, I believe there is a profoundly simple explanation to all of this. The reason that Daniel did not write anything about the Roman Era was because God foreknew that a yet future book was going to be written that corresponded to that Roman Age. In having Daniel acknowledge a Roman Age that would correspond to the "legs of iron," and then excluding it from the rest of Daniel, there is a tacit acknowledgement that another book must be written to fill the gap. In other words, the kingdom represented in the "legs of iron" (Roman Empire) was purposely excluded from the book of Daniel because God foreknew another book – the entire New Testament – was yet to be written. This would then explain why the book of Daniel was a sealed book (Daniel 12:4). Daniel was given incomplete information. He was not provided the Roman catalog of Bible prophecy.

Unlike the sealed book of Daniel, the book of Revelation was unsealed. John is told in Revelation 22:10 to unseal the prophecies of Revelation. In light of the fact the book of Revelation is a distinctively Roman catalog of prophecies that exclusively deal with the Roman

Age, it makes perfect sense for the book to remain unsealed since it literally unseals the Era that Daniel did not know.

This would also explain why the "body" of the fourth beast is never described in Daniel 7. It is not described because *it* had already been described. God foreknew the book of Revelation was going to be written, and contained within this book would be the very "body" of the beast that Daniel saw destroyed in Daniel 7:11.

This empire skip is represented two additional times in the book of Daniel. The first time is in Daniel 8:8-9.

> Therefore the he goat waxed very great: and when he was strong, the great horn was broken; and four notable ones toward the four winds of heaven. And out of one of them came forth a little horn, which waxed exceeding great, toward the south, and toward the east, and toward the pleasant land. (Daniel 8:8-9)

After the "great horn" (Alexander) is "broken" (dies) in verse 8, four notable horns arise in Alexander's place. These four notable horns represent the four generals who each took control over one division of Alexander's vast empire under the "Partition of Babylon". These four notable horns represent Cassander, Lysimachus, Seleucid, and Ptolemy.

Beginning in Daniel 8:9 though, Daniel sees a "little horn" arise from inside one of Alexander's four generals kingdoms. This "little horn" represents a specific advent of the infamous Antichrist rising to power from inside one of these four divisions of the Greek Empire.

In Daniel 8:25 we are told how this "little horn" will "stand up against the Prince of princes" but shall be broken without hand. The "Prince of princes" in this passage is an allusion to the Messiah, Jesus Christ. In the same way that Jesus destroys the fourth beast in Daniel 7:11, Jesus will also destroy the "little horn" in Daniel 8:9. Judging from the context, it appears the fourth beast of Daniel 7 symbolically corresponds to the "little horn" in Daniel 8:9.

If the "little horn" of Daniel 8:9 is the fourth beast, then what happened to the Roman Age that preceded the final 3.5 year empire under the Antichrist?

The second time this empire skip occurs is in Daniel chapter 11. Daniel chapter 11 is quite amazing. None of the things written about in Daniel 11 had come to pass in Daniel's day, yet everyone of them through verse 35 have come to pass with total accuracy. The only reason we cannot state the entire chapter has come to pass is because Daniel 11:36-45 is still future.

Daniel 11:28-35 is a prophecy directed toward the wicked Greek king Antiochus Epiphanes. Now, Epiphanes died in 164 B.C., however the text of Daniel 11:36 continues as if the "king who shall do according to his will" is simply another Greek king who follows after Epiphanes. But it's not, this king in verse 36 represents a particular advent of the Antichrist during the final 3.5 year kingdom. Once again, the book of Daniel "telescopes" forward from the Greek Age in verse 35 to the final 3.5 year age under the Antichrist in verse 36. Where is the Roman Age?

Not only that, but what exactly is it about the Roman Era that makes it so unique? Why is the Roman Age separated from among the other four kingdoms of Babylon, Medo-Persia, Greece, and the final 3.5 year kingdom under Antichrist?

One particularly unique aspect of the Roman Age that makes it so special concerns the passage of Jeremiah 31:31. We know the prophet Jeremiah prophesied about a unique time in which God would cut a new covenant with Israel and the Jewish people.

> Behold, the days come, saith the LORD, that I will make a new covenant with the house of Israel, and with the house of Judah: Not according to the covenant that I will make with the house of Israel; After those days, saith the LORD, I will put my law in their inward parts, and write it in their hearts; and will be their God, and they shall be my people. And they shall no more teach every man his neighbor, and every man his brother, saying, Know the LORD: for they shall all know me, from the least of them unto the greatest,

saith the LORD; for I will forgive their iniquity, and I will remember their sin no more. (Jeremiah 31:31-34)

This new covenant that was cut with Israel and the Jewish people is a covenant which would grant them total and complete atonement from their sins, and therefore allow each of them a direct relationship with God. This covenant was a promise of atonement provided they repent of their sins and acknowledge the Jewish Messiah, Jesus Christ, as their Savior.

Note how the Old and New Testament accounts are configured on the image in Daniel 2.

Five elements presented in Daniel 2:
1. Head of Gold (Old Testament)
2. Chest and Arms of Silver (Old Testament)
3. Belly and Thighs of Brass (Old Testament)
4. Legs of Iron (New Testament)
5. Feet and Toes of Iron and Clay (Old Testament)

If you cross-reference the book of Daniel with the book of Revelation, you will notice how a similar configuration emerges.

Five elements presented in Daniel 2
1. Head of Gold (book of Daniel)
2. Chest and Arms of Silver (book of Daniel)
3. Belly and Thighs of Brass (book of Daniel)
4. Legs of Iron (book of Revelation)
5. Feet and Toes of Iron and Clay (book of Daniel)

When the final Ptolemaic ruler, Cleopatra VII, committed suicide on August 12, 30 B.C., the Greek Hellenistic Era ended and the Roman Era began. In order to understand exactly what the fourth beast in Daniel 7 is, we must examine the Roman Era that precedes the fourth beast of Daniel 7. And in doing this, we must carefully examine the New Testament book of Revelation that reveals the specific identity of the fourth beast.

CHAPTER 2:

BEAST 4:

<u>WHEN SATAN WAS</u>
(2 B.C. – 33 A.D.)

> And it came to pass in those days, that there went out a decree from
> Caesar Augustus, that all the world should be taxed. (Luke 2:1)

Although the Roman Era officially began with the death of Cleopatra
in 30 B.C., the New Testament intimates that the most significant
event marking the Roman Era's inception occurred the moment Caesar
Augustus taxed the world. One of the reasons this decree is so
significant is because the book of Revelation relates how it fulfills the
time when Satan stood before Israel to kill her Messiah as soon as He
was born.

> And there appeared a great wonder in heaven; a woman clothed with
> the sun, and the moon under her feet, and upon her head a crown of
> twelve stars: And she being with child cried, travailing in birth, and
> pained to be delivered. And there appeared another wonder in
> heaven; and behold a great red dragon, having seven heads and ten
> horns, and seven crowns upon his heads. And his tail drew a third
> part of the stars of heaven, and did cast them to the earth: and the
> dragon stood before the woman which was ready to be delivered, for
> to devour her child as soon as it was born. (Revelation 12:1-4)

At this point you may be asking yourself, "What does a Roman census have to do with Satan trying to kill Jesus as soon as he was born?"

The answer may surprise you, but it had everything to do with it. The simple fact of the matter is, if Augustus had never issued this decree that caused the census, Mary and Joseph would never have traveled from Nazareth to Bethlehem. After all, Mary was very pregnant at the time of their journey.

> And Joseph also went up from Galilee, out of the city of Nazareth, into Judaea, unto the city of David, which is called Bethlehem; (because he was of the house and lineage of David:) To be taxed with Mary his espoused wife, being great with child. (Luke 2:4-5)

The reason that Jesus was born in Bethlehem, and not Nazareth, came about as a direct result of the Augustan Census.

So what does this have to do with Satan trying to kill Jesus? Once again, it has everything to do with it. After all, this isn't the first time Satan provoked a king to take a census. More than 900 years before this census, Satan stood up against Israel and provoked King David to take a census.

> And Satan stood up against Israel, and provoked David to number Israel. And David said to Joab and to the rulers of the people, Go, number Israel from Beersheba even to Dan; and bring the number of them to me, that I may know it. (1 Chronicles 21:1)

The reason that Satan provoked King David to take a census was so that he would know the number of Israel. The reason Satan provoked Caesar Augustus is no different in Luke 2:1. Only, in the case of Augustan census, the number of "them" Satan wanted to know was not necessarily "all" of Israel, it was specifically those from the tribe of David, the tribe from which the book of Isaiah prophecies the Messiah would be born.

And in that day there shall be a root of Jesse, which shall stand for an ensign of the people; to it shall the Gentiles seek: and his rest shall be glorious. (Isaiah 11:10)

In the years leading up to Christ's birth, Satan was fully aware that He was about to be born. The only thing that Satan did not know was where it would take place. In provoking Caesar Augustus to take a world-wide census, Satan was guaranteed that all Jewish people from the tribe of David would be gathered in Bethlehem.

Instead of having to stumble across all of Israel to locate the Messiah, all Satan had to do was provoke Augustus, thereby making it easier to locate and kill ("devour") the Messiah.

And there appeared another wonder in heaven; and behold a great red dragon, having seven heads and ten horns, and seven crowns upon his heads. And his tail drew the third part of the stars of heaven, and did cast them to the earth: and the dragon stood before the woman which was ready to be delivered, for to devour her child as soon as it was born. (Revelation 12:3-4)

Ultimately, Satan used King Herod to execute his evil design. When Herod realized he had unsuccessfully schemed in having the wise men reveal where Jesus was, he sent forth his army to slay all children 2 years old and under.

Then Herod, when he saw that he was mocked of the wise men, was exceeding wroth, and sent forth, and slew all the children that were in Bethlehem, and in all the coasts thereof, from two years old and under, according to the time which he had diligently inquired of the wise men. (Matthew 2:16)

Matthew 2:12 relates how Jesus was spared from this horrible tragedy as a result of a divinely inspired dream God provided Joseph. God warned him to flee Bethlehem for Egypt with his family prior to Herod's wrath.

Although the symbolism of Revelation 12:1-4:

And there appeared a great wonder in heaven; a woman clothed with the sun, and the moon under her feet, and upon her head a crown of twelve stars: And she being with child cried, travailing in birth, and pained to be delivered. And there appeared another wonder in heaven; and behold a great red dragon, having seven heads and ten horns, and seven crowns upon his heads. And his tail drew the third part of the stars of heaven, and did cast them to the earth: and the dragon stood before the woman which was ready to be delivered, for to devour her child as soon as it was born. (Revelation 12:1-4)

Relates the events of Luke 2:1-6:

And it came about in those days, that there went out a decree from Caesar Augustus, that all the world should be taxed. (And this taxing was first made when Cyrenius was governor of Syria.) And all went to be taxed, every one to his own city. And Joseph also went up from Galilee, out of the city of Nazareth, into Judaea, unto the city of David, which is called Bethlehem; (because he was of the house and lineage of David:) To be taxed with Mary his espoused wife, being great with child. (Luke 2:1-6)

The passages of Revelation 12:1-4 also fulfill a prophecy found in the texts of Revelation 17:8,11.

The beast that thou sawest was, and is not; and shall ascend out of the bottomless pit, and go into perdition: and they that dwell upon the earth shall wonder, whose names were not written in the book of life from the foundation of the world, when they behold the beast that was, and is not, and yet is. (Revelation 17:8)

And the beast that was, and is not, even he is the eighth, and is of the seven, and goeth into perdition. (Revelation 17:11)

The passages of Revelation 17:8,11 fulfill the prophecy in Revelation 12:1-4 concerning when Satan "was" on earth.

THE BOOK OF REVELATION

Before I begin examining how the passages of Revelation 12:1-4 fulfill that time when the scarlet-colored beast "was" in Revelation 17:8,11, it is important to address when exactly "was" was. In order to do this, it is important to address some background information concerning the book of Revelation.

The author of the book was a man named John. Most scholars believe the John in question is the same John who wrote the Gospel of John. There are some, however, who dispute this claim and believe this John is some other wholly unidentifiable person. Regardless of which camp you fall into, the vast majority of Bible scholars seem to agree this John was a Jewish exile who penned the book on the isle of Patmos, Greece. This is an important point because the place from which he wrote, and the year during which he wrote serve as one of the crucial points of distinction between the book of Revelation and book of Daniel. While the book of Daniel was written by a Jewish exile of Babylon, the book of Revelation was written by a Jewish exile of Rome.

There has also been much speculation concerning when the book of Revelation was written. The reason the dating of the book is so important is because there are a profuse number of grammatical tenses and personal pronouns employed. For instance, when the angel offers John the interpretation of the scarlet-colored beast in Revelation 17:8, the angel explains that the scarlet-colored beast "was, is not, and yet is." In order to determine what these tenses relate, it is critical that the book be dated. If you don't know what year "was" or "is" relate, then it would be rather difficult to ascertain what the vision portrays. According to most Bible experts, the book of Revelation was written around the year 95 A.D.

Much like Daniel, John of Patmos was aided by an angel that was offering him the interpretation of the visions he was receiving. Much of the time these interpretations were offered as the visions were unfolding before him. The vision of Revelation 17:3 is one such case.

So he carried me away in the spirit into the wilderness: and I saw a woman sit upon a scarlet-colored beast, full of names of blasphemy, having seven heads and ten horns. (Revelation 17:3)

This "he" that carries John away "in the spirit into the wilderness" is described in Revelation 17:1 as one of the seven angels which had the seven vials. Since the seven vials are not poured out until all seven seals are opened, it appears as if this vision pertains to the time of the very end.

Unlike the four beasts of Daniel 7:4-7, this scarlet-colored beast in Revelation 17 does not rise up out of the sea. Instead, it is seen occupying a wilderness.

Now, regardless of how one chooses to interpret this vision, based on the fact this scarlet-colored beast is seen in a "wilderness" as opposed to the "sea", it is obvious this scarlet-colored beast is being contrasted against the beasts of Daniel 7:4-7 and Revelation 13:1-2, all of whom rise up out of the sea. Based on the fact the texts of Daniel 7:17 defines how the four beasts in Daniel 7:4-7 represent four human kings, clues us into the idea this scarlet-colored beast of the wilderness probably does not indicate human origin.

The beast that thou sawest was, and is not; and shall ascend out of the bottomless pit, and go into perdition: and they that dwell on the earth shall wonder, whose names were not written in the book of life from the foundation of the world, when they behold the beast that was, and is not, and yet is. (Revelation 17:8)

Note the use of the tenses employed. Concerning the past we know that the scarlet-colored beast of Revelation 17 "was."

Concerning the future, we also know that around the time the book of Revelation was written, the scarlet-colored beast "is not."

Since the book of Revelation was written around 95 A.D., we know this scarlet-colored beast "was" at some point in time before then, while at the time John was writing the book of Revelation he "is not".

Scarlet-colored Beast of Revelation 17:
1. "Was" before (95 A.D.) the book of Revelation was written
2. "Is not" while (95 A.D.) the book of Revelation is being written

According to Revelation 17:8, we also know that two events will occur in the future that will identify who this scarlet-colored beast is. Firstly, we know that it will "ascend out of the bottomless pit." Secondly, we know that when all those whose names are not written in the Book of Life behold the beast, they "shall wonder at him." The prophetic fulfillment of these two prophecies regarding the scarlet-colored beast will play a crucial role in establishing exactly who, what, where, and when this beast shall be.

WHEN THE BEAST OF REVELATION 17 "WAS"

The beast that thou sawest was, and is not; and shall ascend out of the bottomless pit, and go into perdition: and they that dwell on the earth shall wonder, whose names were not written in the book of life from the foundation of the world, when they behold the beast that was, and is not, and yet is. (Revelation 17:8)

And the beast that was, and is not, even he is the eighth, and is of the seven, and goeth into perdition. (Revelation 17:11)

Since the book of Revelation was written sometime around 95 A.D., one can logically deduce that John's vision relating when this beast "was" must have occurred sometime before the year 95 A.D.

Is there any mention of a scarlet-colored beast having seven heads and ten horns in the Bible before the year 95 A.D.? The answer is yes. While the *scarlet-colored* beast of Revelation 17 is not described in precise terminology, it does have a striking resemblance to the great *red* dragon of Revelation 12.

And there appeared another wonder in heaven; and behold a great red dragon having seven heads and ten horns, and seven crowns upon his heads. (Revelation 12:3)

Is this beast scarlet-colored? Yes, it's red.

Does it have seven heads? Yes.

How about ten horns? Yes.

Is the great red dragon identified? Yes.

And the great red dragon was cast out, that old serpent called the Devil, and Satan, which deceiveth the whole world. (Revelation 12:9)

This dragon is none other than the infamous Satan.

Since I have already outlined how the time when Satan "was" began in Luke 2:1, when Caesar Augustus issued a census, a question arises as to exactly when this census was issued.

WHEN WAS THE AUGUSTAN CENSUS?

There has been much speculation concerning when this census went forth. One of the primary obstacles Biblical historians have had in trying to locate this census is that Augustus issued so many of them. In fact, history records that Augustus was very proud of the fact he issued so many censuses, even listing them among his greatest achievements before his death in 14 A.D.

History relates that Augustus's first worldwide census was issued around 8 B.C. He then went on to issue another in 6 B.C. While most Bible scholars argue between these two censuses, the same problem can be cited for both of them. The problem is that the Augustan census could not have occurred more than two years before Christ's birth. If the decree of Luke 2 is the census that Augustus issued in 8 B.C., then Christ would have been close to thirty-seven years of age in the fifteenth year of Tiberius Caesar's reign.

According to Luke 3:1,23, Christ "began to be about thirty years of age" around the fifteenth year of Tiberius Caesar's reign. The fifteenth year of Tiberius's reign fell inside the year 29 A.D. If Christ was "around thirty years of age" in the fifteenth year of Tiberius's reign, then by virtue of the fact the census was issued before His birth, it's most likely this census was issued around Julian year 1-2 B.C.

The key problem in trying to locate a 1-2 B.C. census is that, according to Matthew 2, King Herod was reigning in Jerusalem when Christ was born. Since most historians date the death of King Herod at 4 B.C., this presents a formidable challenge in reconciling Luke's account of Christ being near age 30 (instead of 35) in 29 A.D. The problem that must be reconciled is, how can Christ be thirty years of age in 29 A.D. when most historians date the death of Herod in 4 B.C.?

Some critics will argue the answer rather simple: King Herod did not die in 4 B.C., he died between 2 B.C. and 1 A.D. The principal reason most historians date King Herod's death in 4 B.C. is because the works of a Jewish historian by the name of Josephus records Herod's death occurred in that year. Josephus writes that after Herod captured Jerusalem in 37 B.C., he lived another 34 years, implying his death occurred in 3–4 B.C. The problem with Josephus's account, however, is that Josephus was a Jewish historian who lived from 37–100 A.D., therefore he is not giving an eyewitness account, only a historical one. Of course, the same could be argued of Luke, who many believe died around the same time as Josephus. I suppose the actual question is, whose account do you believe: Luke's or Josephus's?

While historians will forever argue these points, there is indisputable evidence that a decree very similar to the census account offered in Luke 2:1 was given by Caesar Augustus. This decree was given on February 5, 2 B.C. It is better known as the bestowal of "Pater Patriae" (Father of Our Country). Caesar Augustus became deified by the

Roman Senate on this day. Interestingly, this date fell on the Hebrew calendar date 1 Adar. This is significant because Hebrew literature acknowledges this date corresponds to the "plague of darkness" that fell upon Egypt in Exodus 10:21–29 nearly 2000 years before Augustus.

Decree of Augustus in Luke 2:1
Pater Patriae issued February 5, 2 B.C. (Hebrew date 1 Adar)?

On the surface, this decree appears like nothing more than an attempt by the Roman Empire to generate more wealth. However, what was going on behind the scenes was even more interesting. This February 5, 2 B.C. decree not only included a census, but an oath of allegiance to all its Roman members (Israel included). This oath called for all citizens to acknowledge the deity of Augustus. This, of course, greatly disturbed the Jewish Pharisees and Sadducees. Many Israeli citizens revolted, and, according to Acts 5:36-37, many false prophets who boasted themselves to be somebody seemingly arose out of nowhere.

Now most of these false prophets were Israeli citizens. But what makes this sudden phenomenon of false prophets so interesting is that, according to Revelation 12:4, Satan was not alone on earth.

SATAN WAS NOT ALONE

And his [Satan's] tail drew the third part of the stars of heaven, and did cast them to the earth, and the dragon stood before the woman which was ready to be delivered, for to devour her child as soon as it was born. (Revelation 12:4)

According to Revelation 12:4, Satan forced one third of the "stars" to the earth. The "stars" represent all of his fallen angels.

The fallen angels were forcibly cast to the earth by Satan himself. This is symbolically represented in Revelation 12:4 when Satan (using his tail) casts them to the earth.

Is it possible there is connection between the sudden rise of false prophets in Israel, and the convergence of Satan's fallen angels on earth? If you consider the fact that Satan's sole purpose in provoking Caesar Augustus to execute this census was in order to locate Christ, I do not think it's unreasonable to presume that demonic activity would be particularly heavy in Israel. Note how one of these infamous false prophets named Judas (not Iscariot) rose up in Galilee, Christ's homeland.

Beginning in Luke 4:1, the text picks up around thirty years into Christ's life, while Satan is still on earth:

> And Jesus being full of the Holy Ghost returned from Jordan, and was led by the spirit into the wilderness, Being forty days tempted of the devil. (Luke 4:1-2)

Note where Satan tempted Christ: in the wilderness. This tempting by Satan took place around 30 A.D.

The texts of Revelation 17:8,11 states how, at some future point in time, this scarlet-colored beast who "was" no longer "is". This brings up the question, when did Satan go from the beast that "was" to the beast that "is not"?

WHEN SATAN WENT FROM "WAS" TO "IS NOT"

> Now is the judgment of this world: now shall the prince of this world be cast out. (John 12:31)

The "prince of this world" refers to Satan. Satan is described as being "cast out." When Christ relates that the "prince of this world shall be cast out," He is literally conveying a future time when Satan will be cast out of the earth.

So when did this happen?

If you continue reading John 12:32–33, you will notice that Christ specifically referred to His death.

> And I, if I be lifted up from the earth, will draw all men unto me. This he said, signifying what death he should die. (John 12:32-33)

If you apply the "death he should die" to His crucifixion, Jesus is actually prophesying that the moment He dies, Satan will be cast out of the earth.

Jesus Christ was crucified at the age of thirty-three years old during the nineteenth year of Tiberius Caesar's reign. The death of Christ in 33 A.D. corresponds to the time Satan was cast out of the earth.

Therefore, when examining the texts of Revelation 17:8,11 together with the symbols of Revelation 12:1–5, one could presume how these allusions specifically encompass that when Satan "was" on earth between Caesar Augustus's taxing and Christ's death. And since the decree from Augustus was issued in 2 B.C., and Christ's death took place in 33 A.D., these years span 2 B.C. - 33 A.D.

When Satan "was" on earth
2 B.C. - 33 A.D.

THE SIGNIFICANCE OF THE SEVEN CROWNS

Perhaps the most important feature regarding the vision of the great red dragon in Revelation 12:3 is the seven crowns that adorn his seven heads.

> And there appeared another wonder in heaven; and behold a great red dragon having seven heads and ten horns, and *seven crowns upon his heads*. (Revelation 12:3) [italics mine]

What is the significance of the crowns on his seven heads? In order to understand this, it is important to highlight the interpretation related in Revelation 17:10.

> And there are seven kings: five are fallen, and one is, and other is not yet come; and when he cometh, he must continue a short space. (Revelation 17:10)

If the "scarlet-colored" beast of Revelation 17 is a coded way of describing the great "red" dragon in Revelation 12, then the fact the great red dragon possesses seven crowns upon his seven heads is a clear symbolic reference to the seven kings of Revelation 17:10.

Seven Crowns on seven heads of great red dragon
Relate to seven kings outlined in Revelation 17:10

Since the dominant figure of Revelation 12 is Satan, the only way to identify who these seven individual kings are is to frame it within the context of Satan himself.

While I have already established a connection between Satan and Caesar Augustus (via the Augustan census in Luke 2:1), and the context of this connection specifically refers to Satan on earth, a question arises as to whether or not any more connections can be established between Satan on earth and individual kings.

It has also been established how the passages of Revelation 12:1–5 refer to Satan's earthly manifestation between the years 2 B.C. – 33 A.D., one time frame that can be utilized to establish any additional connections would fall between those years.

When Caesar Augustus died in the year 14 A.D., he was succeeded by Tiberius Caesar. The text of Luke 3:1 picks up fifteen years later around 29 A.D.

> Now in the fifteenth year of the reign of Tiberius Caesar. (Luke 3:1)

This passage is the only direct reference made to Tiberius Caesar in the entire Bible. Tiberius Caesar reigned as king of the Roman Empire from 14 A.D. – 37 A.D. The fifteenth year of Tiberius reign would place the text of Luke 3:1 sometime between the years 29–30 A.D.

History records that around the time of 26 A.D. Tiberius was no longer reigning in the city of Rome. According to most historical accounts, Tiberius went on a self-imposed exile to the island of Capri. He never again returned to Rome. Speculation abounds as to what Tiberius was doing in Capri; most of it sensational in tone, but the citizens of Rome were very displeased by his absence.

Beginning in Luke 4:1, the account begins where Satan tempted Christ in the "wilderness" (traditionally believed to be Mount Quarantania). It is here that we can pinpoint Satan's earthly manifestation during the reign of Tiberius.

Since historical records indicate that Tiberius was not residing in the city of Rome during the fifteenth year of his reign in 29 A.D., it is conceivable the Roman Empire was prepared to receive another king. This is significant because it was during this precise year that Satan offered Christ the power and glory of all the kingdoms of the world.

> And the devil, taking him up into a high mountain, shewed unto him all the kingdoms of the world in a moment of time. And the devil said unto him, All this power I will give thee, and the glory of them: for that is delivered unto me; and to whomsoever I will give it. If thou therefore wilt worship me, all shall be thine. (Luke 4:5–7)

This passage clearly intimates that Satan is "delivered" a power and glory over all the kingdoms of the world. Does Satan possess such a power? Was this power that was "delivered" unto Satan exclusively limited to the moment he tempted Christ? Would Satan have delivered this power and glory to Christ if He had worshiped Satan? Is this kingdom that Satan would have delivered to Christ the Roman Empire?

Satan certainly possesses the power to influence kings, as demonstrated in Luke 2:1 and 1 Chronicles 21:1. Did Satan influence Tiberius Caesar to flee Rome for Capri in 26 A.D.? If Satan did influence Tiberius in this way, was he preparing the way for Christ?

Of course these questions will never be answered because, when Satan offers Christ the power to rule over all the kingdoms of the world in exchange that He bow down and worship him, Christ not only refuses but scoffs at the offer in Luke 4:8.

> And Jesus answered and said unto him, Get thee behind me, Satan: for it is written, Thou shalt worship the Lord thy God, and only him shalt thou serve. (Luke 4:8)

While the texts of Luke 4:5–8 pose some challenging questions regarding the extent of Satan's power, the fact that Tiberius Caesar was a king while Satan was still present on earth is not questionable.

Both Caesar Augustus and Tiberius Caesar were kings while Satan was manifest on earth between 2 B.C. -33 A.D. Note how both of them can only be referenced as a direct result of identifying when Satan was on earth. Without deciphering the riddle of Revelation 17:8,11, Augustus and Tiberius and wholly unidentifiable.

Is it mere coincidence these two kings are Roman? Consider for a moment the texts of Revelation 17:8,11, which relate that there is a distinct point in time when Satan "is not":

> The beast that thou sawest *was and is not.* (Revelation 17:8)

> And the beast that *was, and is not.* (Revelation 17:11)

After cross-referencing these passages against Revelation 17:10, note how the king who "is" specifically relates to a sixth.

> And there are seven kings: five are fallen, and *one is.* (Revelation 17:10) [italics mine]

At the time John was writing the book of Revelation in 95 A.D., the Roman Emperor Domitian was reigning as king. Since five of the seven kings will have already died by the time John was writing the book of Revelation, and the sixth king "is" can only be Domitian.

Note the common thread that binds Caesar Augustus, Tiberius Caesar, and Domitian is Satan. Each is identifiable as a direct result of determining when Satan "was" and "is not" on earth.

When Satan "was" on earth
Caesar Augustus and Tiberius Caesar were kings

When Satan "is not" on earth
Domitian is king

All three of these kings are Roman. Is it mere coincidence John of Patmos, a Jewish exile of Rome, is relating the prophecies that specifically apply to Roman kings?

Note how Daniel, a Jewish exile of Babylon specifically identifies kings who established their empires in the city of Babylon.

Kings of Rome
1. Caesar Augustus (John relates)
2. Tiberius (John relates)
3. Domitian (John relates)

Kings of Babylon
1. Nebuchadnezzar (Daniel relates)
2. Cyrus (Daniel relates)
3. Alexander (Daniels relates)

QUICK REVIEW

Up to this point, we have revealed four beasts. The first three beasts of Daniel 7:4–6 and the scarlet-colored beast of Revelation 17:3. In chronological order they are:

Beast 1 (Daniel 7:4) - Nebuchadnezzar (605 B.C. – 562 B.C.)

Beast 2 (Daniel 7:5) - Cyrus (539 B.C. – 529 B.C.)

Beast 3 (Daniel 7:6) - Alexander (336 B.C. – 323 B.C.)

Beast 4 (Revelation 17:3) – Satan (2 B.C. – 33 A.D.)

MAJOR ISSUE WITH REVELATION 12:1–5

Perhaps the most important issue that arises regarding my interpretation of Revelation 12:1–5 is the obvious one which intimates that there is a distinct point in time when Satan was and is not on earth. While I conclude that this particular manifestation of Satan on earth was limited to the years of 2 B.C. – 33 A.D., this conclusion does not pre-suppose this was Satan's only earthly manifestation. In other words, the interpretation of Revelation 12:1–5 only applies to a unique manifestation of Satan on earth, or more specifically, Satan's last manifestation on earth before the year 2008. The fact that there are numerous texts which support Satan manifesting himself on earth long before Augustus's taxing is not lost on me. While Revelation 12:1–5 highlights a particular manifestation, this manifestation was by no means singular.

However, it is very important to note that, while this earthly manifestation was not singular, it is unique in that this particular manifestation of Satan on earth occurred at a time when the Roman Empire was establishing itself on the world scene. From a purely prophetic standpoint, perhaps this is what makes this particular manifestation so unique. Not only was Satan on earth, but it coincided with the precise time during which the Roman Empire establishing itself, and the Messiah's birth.

Furthermore, this earthly manifestation was unique in that all of Satan's fallen angels accompanied him on earth during this time. The reason Satan forced all of his demonic hordes to earth during this time only serves to underscore the enormous magnitude of Christ's birth. Considering the possibility that Christ's death appears to have directly resulted in Satan's expulsion from the earth, it is certainly reasonable to presume that Satan recognized the enormous impact Christ's life would have on the earth. As a result, Satan forced all his fallen angels to earth before and during the time of His life.

Again, there is evidence of Satan being on earth long before 2 B.C. in the Old Testament. Going all the way back to the Garden of Eden, and especially during the life of Job, it can be easily proven from scripture that Satan was manifest on the earth long before 2 B.C. This interpretation is in no way intended to negate the possibility that Satan was on earth before Augustus's taxing in Luke 2:1.

If Satan is the beast that "was, and is not", then what is this evil that saturates the earth today? According to 1 John 4:3, the "spirit of antichrist" is now in the world. If the "spirit of antichrist" is now in the world, then where does it originate? It obviously cannot originate from God? If not God, then who? It seems only logical that this spirit of antichrist derives from Satan himself. But does this mean that Satan possesses a spirit? While it would be highly presumptuous of me to definitively state I fully grasp what is being related regarding the "spirit of antichrist," the abstract notion that it originates from Satan does not seem the least bit far-fetched. After all, Satan is the most powerful entity that God ever created.

CHAPTER 3:

THE SEVEN KINGS

And here is the mind which hath wisdom. The seven heads are seven mountains, on which the woman sitteth. And there are seven kings: five are fallen, and one is, and the other is not yet come; and when he cometh, he must continue a short space. (Revelation 17:9-10)

When I first began studying Bible prophecy, one of the first questions that presented itself was, who are the seven kings of Revelation 17:10? While most pre-millennial scholars settled for the "kingdom" interpretation (Egypt, Assyria, Babylon, Medo-Persia, Greece, Rome, and the Revived Roman Empire), it was pretty clear to me that, from a straight-forward reading of Revelation 17:10, these seven kings actually represent seven individual kings.

The Greek text of Revelation 17:10 supports this conclusion. The Greek word *basilieus* is utilized for the word "kings," as opposed to the Greek word *basileia* (kingdom). The text of Matthew 22:2 contains both words: king and kingdom. In each case, a different Greek word (*basilieus* for "king" and *basileia* for "kingdom") is employed.

Now the Greek and Hebrew word for "king" occurs 2540 times in the Bible. After scouring the Bible numerous times for any clue regarding these seven kings, I finally realized that the only time frame in which these seven kings could correspond had to parallel with time frame represented in the image of Daniel 2. While this somewhat narrowed the field of possibilities to only those kings who reigned after 605 B.C., it by no means limited it enough. What it does do however, is narrow the type of king for which we should be searching.

The fact that there are only five elements represented in the image of Daniel 2 points to those kings who reigned over the Babylonian, Medo-Persian, Greek, and Roman empires. If you combine this with the fact that John of Patmos exclusively relates Roman kings, the search for our type of king after Alexander's death in 323 B.C. is exclusively directed at the Roman Empire.

THE FIRST SIX KINGS

And there are seven kings: five are fallen, and one is. (Revelation 17:10)

The past and present tenses employed in the text of Revelation 17:10 are the key. The five fallen kings are relating five dead kings. The sixth king who "is" represents the king that was reigning in 95 A.D.

The sixth king who "is" when Satan "is not" on earth is Domitian. The text of Revelation 17:10 indicates a series of five kings who died sometime before the year 95 A.D. Once again, a scriptural cross-reference must be established in order to locate and identify the five fallen kings.

Daniel 7 outlines four great beasts that rise up out of the sea. According to Daniel 7:17, these four beasts are expressly defined as kings. Among these four kings, it is significant that three died before 95 A.D.

These three kings are:
1. Nebuchadnezzar (died 562 B.C.)
2. Cyrus (died 519 B.C.)
3. Alexander (died 323 B.C.)

In order to identify the fourth and fifth kings, we must examine the passages of Revelation 12:1–5, which encompass a 35 year duration when Satan was on earth between 2 B.C. to 33 A.D. Since the two kings that reigned inside this window were Caesar Augustus and Tiberius Caesar, we now have five fallen kings.

The sixth king who reigned after Satan was cast out of the earth in 33 A.D. is Domitian. The identity of the five fallen kings and the sixth king in Revelation 17:10 can now be identified.

Five fallen kings and Sixth king who "is"
1. Nebuchadnezzar (died 562 B.C.)
2. Cyrus (died 519 B.C.)
3. Alexander (died 323 B.C.)
4. Caesar Augustus (when Satan "was" on earth between 2 B.C. – 33 A.D.)
5. Tiberius Caesar (when Satan "was" on earth between 2 B.C. – 33 A.D.)
6. Domitian (when Satan "is not" on earth after 33 A.D. – Present)

HISTORY AS A FORESHADOW OF THE FUTURE

Bible prophecy at its most fundamental level is a guide that can be utilized to relate specific information about the future. This is why the fascination with Bible prophecy has persisted for so many centuries. Unfortunately, the methods employed for revealing these events has oftentimes been exploited by individuals who have no idea how to relate them.

The biblical method of interpretation employs a technique very similar to the literary device of *foreshadowing*. Foreshadowing is a literary device that is primarily used to subtly hint at a future event before it actually occurs.

Perhaps the most famous literary example of foreshadowing occurs in the tragedy *Romeo and Juliet*. Very early in the tragedy, Romeo and Juliet each proclaim how they would rather die than live without one another. At the time Romeo and Juliet made this declaration, neither had any designs of dying, let alone for one another. However, this sentiment proved prophetic as both later ended up dying as a direct result of their love for each other.

The Bible is very similar in this regard. Unlike literary foreshadowing though, you don't have to finish the book in order to determine where the foreshadowing took place. This is where the Greek methods of biblical interpretation diverge from the kosher Hebraic method of biblical interpretation. The Greek method of Bible prophecy employs a method of interpretation that is focused on prediction/fulfillment, while the Hebraic method employs a more pattern-based method that utilizes the framework of world history to relate future events. In other words, the Hebraic method supports the idea that if you want to know what is going to happen, you must first realize what has already happened.

One of the more prominent examples of the Hebraic method is utilized in the text of Daniel 11:31–32.

> And arms shall stand on his part, and they shall pollute the sanctuary of strength, and shall take away the daily sacrifice, and they shall place the abomination that maketh desolate. And such as do wickedly against the covenant shall he corrupt by flatteries.

Antiochus Epiphanes was a Seleucid ruler who reigned from 175 B.C. until his death in 164 B.C. He has the ignoble distinction of being the sole cause of a massive Jewish uprising known as the Maccabean revolt.

According to some historians, Antiochus Epiphanes was among the first leaders in all of history to subject a nation to religious persecution. After the armies of Epiphanes sacked the city of Jerusalem, Epiphanes defiled the Jewish temple by constructing a statue in honor of the Greek god Zeus. He then demanded the Jewish people worship it. According to many Bible scholars, this incident is what divinely inspired Daniel to write "the abomination that maketh desolate" in the text of Daniel 11:31.

This declaration forcing the Jewish people to worship Zeus not only offended the sensibilities of Israel, but it also offended God Himself. Epiphanes was only able to accomplish all of this after he curried the favor of a small number of prominent Jewish elite.

If any of this sounds familiar to those of you who study Bible prophecy, it is probably because these actions will repeat themselves in the last days under the Antichrist. Only this time it will not exclusively apply to Israel, it will be enforced on a global scale.

FIRST SIX KINGS AS A FORESHADOW OF ANTICHRIST

If this type of prophetic foreshadowing applies to events that have yet to occur, then the first six kings outlined in Revelation 17:10 should prefigure something unique about the future Antichrist. But exactly how do these six kings prefigure the Antichrist? In order to understand this, we must carefully examine the six kings against one another. If you examine them closely, you will notice how peculiar patterns begin to emerge.

Firstly, you will notice that while the first three kings are symbolized in the book of Daniel, the proceeding three kings are represented in the book of Revelation. This raises the question, "How do the first three kings highlighted in the book of Daniel relate to the three kings highlighted in the book of Revelation?"

Book of Daniel
1. Nebuchadnezzar
2. Cyrus
3. Alexander

Book of Revelation
4. Caesar Augustus
5. Tiberius Caesar
6. Domitian

Secondly, you will notice that the first three kings in the book of Daniel established their empires in the city of Babylon, while the proceeding three kings established their capital in Rome. This raises the following question, "How does this Rome-Babylon distinction amongst the six kings relate to the Antichrist?"

Book of Daniel
1. King Nebuchadnezzar (capital: Babylon)
2. Cyrus (capital: Babylon)
3. Alexander (capital: Babylon)

Book of Revelation
4. Caesar Augustus (capital: Rome)
5. Tiberius Caesar (capital: Rome)
6. Domitian (capital: Rome)

Thirdly, notice how the first three kings of Babylon are represented as beasts in Daniel 7:4–6, while the proceeding three Roman kings are not represented as beasts at all. Instead of being represented as beasts, the Roman kings are only identifiable as a direct result of understanding when Satan "was" and "is not" on the earth. How does Satan's connection to these three Roman kings in the book of Revelation relate to three kings highlighted in the book of Daniel?

Book of Daniel
1. Nebuchadnezzar (Beast of Daniel 7:4)
2. Cyrus (Beast of Daniel 7:5)

3. Alexander (Beast of Daniel 7:6)

<u>Book of Revelation</u>
4. Caesar Augustus (when Satan "was" on earth)
5. Tiberius Caesar (when Satan "was" on earth)
6. Domitian (when Satan "is not" on earth)

Finally, you will notice that the three kings of Babylon were related by the Babylonian exile Daniel, while the proceeding three Roman kings were related by the Roman exile John.

<u>Book of Daniel</u>
1. Nebuchadnezzar (Babylonian exile Daniel relates)
2. Cyrus (Babylonian exile Daniel relates)
3. Alexander (Babylonian exile Daniel relates)

<u>Book of Revelation</u>
4. Caesar Augustus (Roman exile John relates)
5. Tiberius Caesar (Roman exile John relates)
6. Domitian (Roman exile John relates)

In order to decipher the information these six kings are foreshadowing about the seventh, we must make a thorough examination of all prophecies concerning this seventh king.

THE SEVENTH KING

And there are seven kings: five are fallen, and one is, and the other is not yet come; and when he cometh, he must continue a short space. (Revelation 17:10)

Revelation 17:10 relates a major prophecy concerning a seventh king that "is not yet come." While most pre-millennial scholars apply the "kingdom" theory to this seventh king, and believe this seventh king represents the Revived Roman Empire (European Union), I believe the interpretation of this seventh king actually applies to an individual man.

While very little information is offered in Revelation 17:10 concerning this seventh king, except that he "is not yet come," there is one distinctive quality that separates this seventh king from the six kings who came before him, and that is the ten kings who are prophesied to reign *together* with him.

Distinctive Quality of Seventh King
Ten kings who reign together with him

Note how the books of Daniel and Revelation both identify a distinct group of ten kings in Daniel 7:24 and Revelation 17:12.

> And the ten horns out of this kingdom are ten kings that shall arise. (Daniel 7:24)

> And the ten horns which thou sawest are ten kings. (Revelation 17:12)

If this group of ten kings represents an identical group, why is it they are related in two separate books? Does this suggest a direct relationship regarding the rules of interpretation that govern the books of Daniel and Revelation? If it does, then perhaps this partially explains why Daniel was told in Daniel 12:4 to "shut up the words, and seal the book." God foreknew that before anyone could decipher the book of Daniel, the book of Revelation must first be written. And since the book of Revelation was written over six-hundred years after the book of Daniel, the book of Daniel had to be sealed.

If a direct relationship regarding the rules of interpretation of both Daniel and Revelation does exist, then perhaps this rule has other applications as well. For instance, when Revelation 17:9 relates that the seven heads represent the seven mountains of Rome, is it possible this interpretation not only applies to the beasts related in the book of Revelation, but the four beasts represented in Daniel 7 as well? If it does, then the fact that none of the four beasts that rise out of the sea in Daniel 7:4-7 possess seven heads must relate to the fact these four beasts are peculiarly non-Roman in some uniquely connected fashion.

Notice how this cross-over effect regarding the rules of interpretation can be applied to the beast of Revelation 13:1-2. When the angel offers Daniel the interpretation regarding the four beasts in Daniel 7:17 as "four kings", is it a coincidence the beast of Revelation 13:1-2 exclusively relates to a king as well? Is it a coincidence the beast of Revelation 13:1-2 also rises out of the sea? Is it a coincidence this seven-headed beast in Revelation 13:1-2 is the only Roman king that rises out of the sea?

This direct relationship between the two books is demonstrably represented in the text of Revelation 13:2, when the Roman Prince that rise from the sea is represented using the exact symbols that relate Nebuchadnezzar, Cyrus, and Alexander.

Roman Prince of Revelation 13:1–2
1. Represented as a "lion" (Daniel 7:4)
2. Represented as a "bear" (Daniel 7:5)
3. Represented as a "leopard" (Daniel 7:6)

Now history bears out that Nebuchadnezzar, Cyrus, and Alexander had little or no connection at all with Roman Kings. After all, how could they if their appearance in history came long before the Roman Empire was established.

But this is where Bible prophecy is a much different instrument than the type of Gnostic interpretation you see today regarding prophecy where people attempt to "predict" the future. When the text of Revelation 13:2 establishes a direct symbolic relationship between the beast of Revelation 13:1-2 and the first three beasts outlined in Daniel 7:4-6, the text is not asking if a relationship does exist, it is inferring that the connection already exists, and that if we are to locate this connection, the only source available to establish it is the Bible itself.

On page 39, I related how the seven crowns on the seven heads of the great red dragon relate to the seven kings outlined in Revelation 17:10. Note how the application of this interpretation not only applies to the great red dragon of Revelation 12, but likewise to the scarlet-colored beast of Revelation 17:3. According to Revelation 17:10, the seventh king "has not yet come." Now, the fact that this seventh king "has not yet come" impacts the interpretation of the ten kings related in Revelation 17:12. If none of the previous six kings ever co-reigned together with ten kings, then it is logical to conclude this seventh king must co-reign together with the ten kings. The texts of Revelation 17:10,12 support the idea.

> And there are seven kings: five are fallen, and one is, *and the other is not yet come*. (Revelation 17:10) [italics mine]

> And the ten horns which thou sawest are ten kings, *which have received no kingdom as yet*. (Revelation 17:12) [italics mine]

Logic dictates that if six of the seven kings have already reigned, and the ten kings have not yet received their kingdom, it stands to reason the ten kings and this seventh king must reign together.

In fact, from a purely theoretical point of view, if the seven heads on the beast of Revelation represent the seven kings of Revelation 17:10, then only one of the seven heads is capable of possessing the ten horns that represent the ten kings. And that head which possesses the ten horns can only apply to the seventh king.

Ten-Horned Head in Book of Revelation
Exclusively applies to the seventh king

If you cross-reference the texts of Daniel 7:7 and Revelation 13:1–2, you will notice that these are the only two beasts in the entire Bible that both rise up out of the sea and possess ten horns. The fact that each of them fulfill both of these conditions is significant because, while the great red dragon of Revelation 12 and scarlet-colored beast of Revelation 17 also possess ten horns, neither of them rises up out of the sea.

Only Beasts that rise out of sea and possess ten horns
1. Beast of Revelation 13:1–2
2. Beast of Daniel 7:7

Since the three beasts that rise up of the sea in Daniel 7:4–6 represent gentile kings Nebuchadnezzar, Cyrus, and Alexander, it follows that the beasts of Daniel 7:7 and Revelation 13:1-2 who rise up out of sea must represent gentile kings as well.

The question that now presents itself is, which one of these beasts represents the seventh king of Revelation 17:10? Theoretically, the possibility exists that either one of them could. In order to draw a clear distinction between them, we must compare them.

COMPARING THE BEASTS OF REVELATION 13:1–2 AND DANIEL 7:7

While it is clear that the beast of Revelation 13:1–2 exclusively represents a Roman king, this is not the case with the beast of Daniel 7:7. Unlike the beast of Revelation 13:1-2, the beast of Daniel 7:7 represents both a "king" (Dan. 7:17) and a "kingdom" (Dan. 7:23).

Key Distinction between beast of Revelation 13:1-2 and Daniel 7:7
1. Beast of Revelation 13:1–2 = King
2. Beast of Daniel 7:7 = King + Kingdom

Another key distinction between the beast of Daniel 7:7 and Revelation 13:1-2 is the number of heads they each possess. Note how the beast of Revelation 13:1-2 possesses seven heads.

> And I stood upon the sand of the sea, and saw a beast rise up out of the sea, having *seven heads* and ten horns. [italics mine]

While the fourth beast of Daniel 7 only possesses one head.

> Then I would know the truth of the fourth beast, which was diverse from all the others, exceedingly dreadful, whose teeth were of iron, and his nails of brass; which devoured, brake in pieces, and stamped the residue with his feet. *And of the ten horns that were in his head.* (Daniel 7:19-20) [italics mine]

One interesting idea regarding the interpretation of these seven heads is found in Revelation 17:9, which relates how they represent the seven mountains of Rome.

If the seven heads literally represent the seven mountains of Rome, then by virtue of the fact that the fourth beast of Daniel 7 only possesses one head should explain something unique about a non-Rome geographical location.

Differing number of heads
Different geographical locations?

Another key distinction between the two beasts is that while the fourth great beast of Daniel 7:7 is seen in "night visions," the beast of Revelation 13:1–2 is not.

> After this I saw in the *night visions*, and behold a fourth beast, dreadful and terrible. (Daniel 7:7) [italics mine]

These "night visions" suggest that the beast of Daniel 7:7 rises to power at a point in time that is distinct from the beast in Revelation 13:1–2.

Night visions in Daniel 7:7
A rise to power at a distinct point in time?

THE TEN HORNS

While these two beasts share three unique differences, it is also true they share one unique quality: the ten horns.

According to Daniel 7:24 and Revelation 17:12, these ten horns represent ten individual kings.

> And the ten horns out of this kingdom are ten kings that shall arise. (Daniel 7:24)

> And the ten horns which thou sawest are ten kings. (Revelation 17:12)

In my opinion, these ten kings represent an identical group.

Since both beasts possess ten horns, and these ten horns represent an identical group, one distinct quality they both share is the ten kings that reign together with them.

Ten Kings of Daniel 7:24 and Revelation 17:12
Will reign together with beast of Revelation 13:1–2 and beast of Daniel 7:7

While both beasts possess ten horns, notice the crucial symbolic distinction that exists between them in Revelation 13:1.

> And I stood upon the sand of the sea, and saw a beast rise up out of the sea, having seven heads and ten horns, *and upon his horns ten crowns*, and upon heads the name of blasphemy. (Revelation 13:1) [italics mine]

While the ten horns on the beast of Revelation 13:1-2 possess ten crowns, the ten horns on the beast of Daniel 7:7 do not.

So what exactly does this represent?

Note in Daniel 7:24 how a chronology is established with respect to the ten kings and the Antichrist that rises to power after them.

And the ten horns out of this kingdom are ten kings that shall arise: and another shall rise after them; and he shall be diverse from the first, and he shall subdue three kings. (Daniel 7:24)

The chronology of Daniel 7:24 states that the ten kings will rise to power before Antichrist. In light of the fact the beast of Revelation 13:1-2 exclusively relates to a king, and its ten horns are adorned with ten crowns, the presence of the ten crowns on the ten horns is extremely significant because it demonstrates how the ten kings have already risen to power. In other words, the presence of the ten crowns demonstrates how the beast of Revelation 13:1-2 is the 11th "diverse" king related in Daniel 7:8,24. Therefore, the relationship between ten crowns on the ten horns of the beast in Revelation 13:1-2 is a chronological one.

Ten Crowns on Ten Horns
Establish how the ten kings have already risen to power

The ten crowns on the ten horns also establish how the beast of Revelation 13:1–2 is the seventh king outlined in Revelation 17:10. By virtue of the fact the ten-horned head exclusively applies to the seventh king, and the ten crowns that adorn the ten horns relate how the ten kings have already risen to power, these two facts together prove how the only king the beast of Revelation 13:1-2 can relate is the seventh one found in Revelation 17:10.

Beast of Revelation 13:1-2
Represents the seventh king of Revelation 17:10

Therefore, it can be stated how the seventh king of Revelation 17:10 is symbolically represented in both the "little horn" of Daniel 7:8 and beast of Revelation 13:1-2.

Seventh King of Revelation 17:10
1. Little Horn of Daniel 7:8,24
2. Beast of Revelation 13:1–2

Now that the seventh king has been established, the interpretation for all seven kings related in Revelation 17:10 can be identified.

Seven Kings of Revelation 17:10
1. Nebuchadnezzar
2. Cyrus
3. Alexander
4. Caesar Augustus
5. Tiberius Caesar
6. Domitian
7. Roman Antichrist

CHAPTER REVIEW

In this chapter, we examined the critical role that history plays in our ability to decipher future events. We examined how history records that none of first six kings of Revelation 17:10 ever reigned together with ten kings. The fact that none of the previous six kings ever co-reigned with ten kings proves how the seventh king of Revelation 17:10 will co-reign together with ten kings.

In comparing the beasts of Revelation 13:1–2 and Daniel 7:7, I attempted to illustrate how they possess three distinct differences and share one unique quality. in that each of them possess ten horns. The three distinct differences between them relate how the beast of Revelation 13:1-2 exclusively relates a king, will rise to power in distinct geographical location, and precede the fourth beast of Daniel 7.

The unique quality they both share is that they co-reign with ten individual kings. This can be demonstrated by cross-referencing the texts of Daniel 7:24 and Revelation 17:12.

While this group of ten kings is identical, they also highlight an additional key distinction between them. The fact that the beast of Revelation 13:1-2 exclusively refers to an individual king, and is symbolized with ten crowns on its ten horns ascribes to the fact this beast is the "diverse" 11th king outlined in Daniel 7:8,24. This proves how the beast of Revelation 13:1-2 is the seventh king of Revelation 17:10.

In the chapter that follows, I will take a closer look at the beast of Revelation 13:1–2. Using the information that I have already acquired about the six kings that precede him, I will carefully examine the additional symbols that highlight the beast of Revelation 13:1-2.

CHAPTER 4:

BEAST 5:

BEAST OF REVELATION 13:1–2 (DAY 1 OF 70TH WEEK – DEADLY WOUND)

And I stood upon the sand of the sea, and saw a beast rise up out of the sea, having seven heads and ten horns, and upon his horns ten crowns, and upon his heads the name of blasphemy. And the beast which I saw was like a leopard, and his feet were as the feet of a bear, and his mouth as the mouth of a lion: And the dragon gave him his power, and his seat, and great authority. (Revelation 13:1–2)

The information in the passage above is foundational for all who are interested in Bible prophecy. The groundwork is being laid for more than a few prophecies concerning the future. While these passages are highly symbolic, it is the application of these symbols that drives the lifeblood of Bible prophecy.

THE ROMAN ANTICHRIST

The Gentile king symbolized in the beast of Revelation 13:1–2 is an allusion to the infamous Antichrist written about in numerous passages throughout the Bible. One such passage is found in Daniel 9:26.

And after threescore and two weeks shall Messiah be cut off, but not for himself: *and the people of the prince that shall come* shall destroy the city and the sanctuary, and the end thereof shall be with a flood, and unto the end of the war desolations are determined. (Daniel 9:26) [italics mine]

In Daniel 9:26, the Antichrist is referred to as "the people of the prince that shall come." The key question that arises from this text is, how can the "people" that define this prince be described?

When the angel Gabriel offered Daniel the interpretation of this passage, Daniel had no idea about the type of kingdom that would succeed Greece. After all, Daniel was only alive to witness the two world empires of Babylon and Medo-Persia. It was amazing enough he was prophesying about a Greek Empire succeeding the Medo-Persians in Daniel 8:21 and Daniel 11.

Of course, the true author of all Bible prophecy is God Himself. In fact, Revelation 19:10 states how the testimony of Jesus is the very spirit of prophecy itself.

While Daniel was never given the opportunity to define the type of kingdom that would succeed the Greek Empire, God made sure that Daniel at least alluded to it. This is how the prophecy of Daniel 9:26 was intended to function: as a testimony to the omnipotence of God Himself.

God instructed the angel Gabriel to tell Daniel how the prince of Daniel 9:26 will be defined within the context of the same people that destroy the Second Temple.

In the year 70 A.D., the future Roman Emperor Titus, along with four Roman Legions, surrounded the city of Jerusalem and burned it to the ground. Along with the destruction of Jerusalem, the Romans also destroyed the Jewish Temple. While Titus is not "the prince that shall come," he certainly fulfilled the prophecy regarding the "people" of this prince that shall come. And since these people who destroyed the city of Jerusalem and the temple were Romans, this prince who shall come must also be Roman.

Now this prophecy was written over five hundred years before Titus and his Roman Legions laid siege to the city of Jerusalem. The fact that this prince who shall come must be Roman, and the beast of Revelation 13:1-2 possesses seven heads, should alert us to the possibility this beast and the prince who shall come represent the same king. According to Revelation 17:9, we are told the seven heads represent seven mountains.

> And here is the mind which hath wisdom, the seven heads are seven mountains. (Revelation 17:9)

Historically, the city of Rome is known as the "seven-hilled city." If the city of Rome is what seven heads of the beast of Revelation 13:1-2 specifically relate, then this might explain how it is related to the prince who shall come in Daniel 9:26.

This begs the question, is there any additional symbolism that accentuates the Roman aspect of the beast in Revelation 13:1-2 ?

THE NAME OF BLASPHEMY

> And I stood upon the sand of the sea, and saw a beast rise up out of the sea, having seven heads and ten horns, and upon his horns ten crowns, *and upon his heads the name of blasphemy.* (Revelation 13:1) [italics mine]

The "name of blasphemy" that appears on all seven heads is extremely significant. The fact that this name appears in the singular tense, and is found in more than one head ("heads"), suggests how it possesses a particularly distinct quality.

In order to determine what this distinctive quality is, we must examine whether or not the seven heads can be defined in a way that is distinct from the definition offered in Revelation 17:10. While Revelation

17:10 relates how the seven heads represent seven kings, note how the text of Revelation 17:9 defines these seven heads as seven mountains as well.

> And here is the mind which hath wisdom. The seven heads are seven mountains, on which the woman sitteth. (Revelation 17:9)

The interpretation of the seven heads outlined in Revelation 17:9 relates how the seven heads can be additionally defined according to seven mountains.

Seven Heads symbolize
1. Seven Mountains
2. Seven Individual Kings

The fact that a [singular tense] "name of blasphemy" appears on the [plural tense] "heads" is significant because the only "name" that can apply to this beast is the literal name of the seventh king. This is what John is relating when he writes how the name of the beast will somehow correspond to the numerical value 666.

> And he causeth all, both small and great, rich and poor, free and bond, to receive a mark in their right hand, or in their foreheads: And that no man might buy or sell, save he that had the mark, or the name of the beast, or the number of his name. Here is wisdom. Let him that hath understanding count the number of the beast: for it is the number of a man; and his number is Six hundred threescore and six. (Revelation 13:16-18)

The fact that John assigns a precise numerical value to this name demonstrates how specific a name it is. It appears as if John had literally witnessed the name of the future Antichrist. But the question that concerns us is, why did John have to witness this one name in all seven heads?

The fact this "name of blasphemy" is written in the singular tense, and the only king to which it could apply is the seventh, automatically rules out the possibility of its significance relates to any of the six kings that preceded the seventh in Revelation 17:10. After all, six of the seven kings are already dead when the seventh king rises to power. Therefore, one application of the "names of blasphemy" in the "heads" is that it applies to the literal name of the Antichrist.

Name of Blasphemy in the Heads
Symbolizes the literal name of Antichrist

Since the seven heads symbolize a dual application of "seven kings" and "seven mountains", a question arises as to how the "name of blasphemy" in the "heads" applies to the seven mountains outlined in Revelation 17:9.

The fact that the beast of Revelation 13:1-2 symbolically represents a Roman king, and his "name" in the heads corresponds to a numerical value that only applies the Antichrist, leads me to conclude the only logical explanation is that the "name of blasphemy" in the "heads" additionally symbolizes the city in which this Antichrist will rise to power: Rome.

Name of Blasphemy in Heads
Symbolizes the city of Rome

DOMINION FROM SATAN

Another important feature concerning the text of Revelation 13:1–2 is the information that relates how this Roman king will derive his power and dominion from Satan.

> And the beast which I saw was like unto a leopard, and his feet were as the feet of a bear, and his mouth the mouth of a lion: *and the dragon gave him his power, and his seat, and his great authority.* (Revelation 13:2) [italics mine]

The "dragon" is defined as Satan in Revelation 12:9. Revelation 13:2 is extremely significant because this is the first time in the history of mankind that any ruler has ever received his dominion absent the authority of God.

The fact that this king's power and dominion is rooted in Satan authority is extremely significant in light of the prophesies concerning the fourth beast of Daniel 7:7. According to Daniel 7:7, the fourth beast is "diverse" from all the beasts that rose to power before him. The fact that the king represented in Revelation 13:1-2 is the first in all of recorded history to receive his authority from Satan fulfills the prophecy regarding the intended meaning of the term "diverse" in Daniel 7:7. When the Roman Antichrist of Revelation 13:1-2 rises to power with a covenant in the city of Rome, this will be the first time in human history that a king has risen to power absent the authority of God.

"Diverse" from Daniel 7:7
Represents Satanic dominion

After applying the interpretation of the word "diverse" to a king and kingdom, it is important to recognize how this fourth beast actually represents both a king and a kingdom whose power is rooted in Satanic dominion.

Fourth Beast of Daniel 7 represents:
1. King who derives dominion from Satan
2. Kingdom that derives dominion from Satan

One of the key distinctions between the beast of Revelation 13:1-2 and beast of Daniel 7:7 is the fact the beast of Revelation 13:1-2 exclusively represents a king. The beast of Revelation 13:1-2 fulfills the vision of the "diverse" king related in Daniel 7:8,24. This "diverse" king fulfills the first of a two-fold conditional prophecy concerning the fourth beast of Daniel 7. The beast of Revelation 13:1-2, therefore, fulfills first part of the two-fold conditional prophecy regarding the beast of Daniel 7:7.

Beast of Revelation 13:1-2
Fulfills first of two conditions concerning the beast of Daniel 7:7

Since the beast of Daniel 7:7 requires that both a diverse king and kingdom come into existence, the fact that the diverse king requirement precedes the diverse kingdom requirement alerts us to the fact the diverse kingdom chronologically arrives after the diverse king.

Diverse Kingdom Requirement
Chronologically occurs after Diverse King

WHEN IS BEAST OF REVELATION 13:1–2?

The text that most pre-millennial scholars utilize to prove when the Roman Prince of Daniel 9:26 rises to power is related in Daniel 9:27.

> And he shall confirm the covenant with many for one week.
> (Daniel 9:27)

The "week" in question is actually referring to one week of years, or seven Hebrew years. One Hebrew year comprises 360 days, so seven years would comprise exactly 3520 days. This final week of years is commonly referred to as "The Seventieth Week of Daniel." According to Daniel 9:27, this seventieth week will begin when the Antichrist confirms a "covenant" with many.

I believe this "he" that confirms the covenant with many represents the same "people of the prince that shall come" in Daniel 9:26. Since we know these "people" were Roman, it follows this prince must be Roman as well. Therefore, since the beast of Revelation 13:1–2 describes the same Roman Prince in Daniel 9:26 who confirms the covenant with many at the beginning of the week, it follows this beast of Revelation 13:1–2 that rises out of the sea will also rise to power with a covenant.

Daniel's Seventieth Week
1. Comprises exactly seven Hebrew years (3520 days)
2. Begins when a Roman Antichrist confirms a covenant

THE COVENANT AND THREE FALLEN KINGS

According to a popular online Dictionary, the word *dominion* is defined as "a territory, usually of considerable size, in which a single rulership holds sway." Of course, the territory over which a king "holds sway" is usually defined according to the land over which he reigns.

But what is the true source of a king or queen's power? According to the Bible, the sole source of a king's power is the dominion he receives from God. Now, this dominion that God bestows upon a king or queen cannot be seen by the naked eye. In spite of this fact, however, within the spiritual world, dominion is just as tangible as the paper you are now reading, if not more so.

The simple fact of the matter is that this piece of paper can cause you no real harm. But the one to whom dominion is given can wreak endless, merciless havoc on all those under whom he reigns.

> I considered the horns, and, behold, there came up among them another little horn, before whom there were three of the first horns plucked up by the roots. (Daniel 7:8)

The text of Daniel 7:8 makes reference to a little horn that "came up." What exactly does the expression "came up" convey? The interpretation is offered in Daniel 7:24:

> And the ten horns out of this kingdom are ten kings that shall arise: and another shall rise after them; and he shall be diverse from the first, and he shall subdue three kings. (Daniel 7:24)

Daniel 7:24 defines these "horns" as individual kings. According to this passages, ten kings must rise to power before the "another" 11th king. In other words, the pre-condition to this 11th "diverse" king's rise to power is that ten "normal" kings must rise to power before him. Logic dictates that if the 11th king is "diverse," and this diversity represents a dominion from Satan, then logic dictates that the first ten kings that rise to power before the "diverse" king must receive their dominion non-diversely (from God).

First ten kings that rise before "diverse" 11th king:
Receive their dominion from God

Therefore, Daniel 7:24 relates that before the Roman Prince can rise to power, ten kings must rise to power before him. These ten kings receive their authority from God. The expression "came up" in Daniel 7:8 specifically relates a rise to power. This little 11th horn that came up after the first ten relates how the Antichrist's rise to power will chronologically arrive after the first ten kings.

What exactly do we know about the Roman Antichrist's rise to power? The text of Daniel 9:27 relates that his rise to power will be marked by a "covenant." This covenant, then, is the key distinguishing characteristic that marks the 11th king's rise to power. This covenant will be the instrument used to establish the Antichrist's authority at the inception of Daniel's 70th Week in the city of Rome.

First Condition of Fourth Beast
Is fulfilled when Antichrist of Revelation 13:1–2 rises to power with a covenant in city of Rome at the beginning of Daniel's 70th Week

> And the ten horns out of this kingdom are ten kings that shall arise: and another [11th king] shall rise after them; and he shall be diverse from the first [ten kings], and he [11th 'diverse' king] shall subdue three kings. (Daniel 7:24)

Notice in Daniel 7:24 how this "subduing" of three kings in Daniel 7:24 is symbolized in Daniel 7:8 as a "plucking up by the roots."

I considered the horns [ten kings], and, behold, there came up among them another little horn [11th diverse king], before whom there were three of the first [ten kings] horns plucked up by the roots. (Daniel 7:8)

The three kings who are "plucked up" takes place simultaneous to the Antichrist's rise to power in Rome. Since we know this rise to power is marked by a covenant, it stands to reason these three kings who are uprooted have been uprooted as a direct result of this covenant.

And since the first ten kings derive their authority from God, the expression "plucking up by the roots" must represent a loss of God-given dominion. The reason these three kings lose their God-given dominion is precisely because they enter into covenant with the Antichrist at the beginning of the 70th Week.

While Daniel 7:8 is relating how three of the ten kings will enter into covenant with the Antichrist, we can deduce that seven of the ten kings will not enter into covenant. As a result of not entering into covenant with the Antichrist, these seven kings will retain their God-given authority.

Now, the conditions calling for the fourth great beast of Daniel 7:7 become a little clearer. We know that three of the ten kings who first rise to power will enter into covenant with the Antichrist. And since the final condition allowing the fourth beast of Daniel 7 to rise to power specifically concerns a kingdom whose dominion is derived from Satan, until the seven remaining kings enter into covenant with the Antichrist, the fourth great beast of Daniel 7:7 cannot rise to power.

Final Condition of Fourth Beast
Is fulfilled when seven remaining kings agree to enter into covenant with Antichrist

OPENING OF FIRST SEAL SIGNALS BEGINNING OF SEVENTIETH WEEK

> And I saw, and behold a white horse: and he that sat on him had a bow; and a crown was given unto him: and he went forth conquering, and to conquer. (Revelation 6:2)

Most pre-millennial scholars believe the opening of the first seal in Revelation 6:2 signals the beginning of Daniel's Seventieth Week related in Daniel 9:27. They see this rider upon the white horse as representing the Antichrist. The fact he wears a crown and possesses a bow seems to support this claim. According to Daniel 8:25 he shall destroy many by peace. Unlike the great kings before him, who conquered through military might, the Roman Antichrist exploits his skillful mind and clever tongue to subdue the nations. The Bereshith has this to say about how the symbol of arrows, or in the case of the bow-wielding rider of Revelation 6:2, the lack thereof.

> Slander is compared to an arrow, not to any other handy weapon, such as a sword, etc., because like an arrow it kills at a distance. It can be uttered in Rome and have its baneful effect in Syria.

The reason the rider of the white horse has no arrows is because they have already gone forth in the form of slander and intimidation. In light of the fact he rises to power with a covenant, it's not difficult to presume how the covenant will be used to achieve his aim of world control.

Opening of first seal in Revelation 6:2
Marks beginning of the seventieth week, when the Antichrist rises to power with a covenant

THE BODY

The most striking aspect about the body of the beast in Revelation 13:1–2 is the direct symbolic connection it has to the three beasts related in Daniel 7:4–6.

And the beast which I saw was like unto a leopard, and his feet were as the feet of a bear, and his mouth as the mouth of a lion: and the dragon gave him his power, and his seat, and great authority. (Revelation 13:2)

Note how these descriptions imply that a direct connection exists between the beasts of Daniel 7:4–6 and the beast of Revelation 13:1–2.

Beast of Revelation 13:1–2
1. Bear (Daniel 7:4)
2. Leopard (Daniel 7:5)
3. Lion (Daniel 7:6)

The fact that this king of Revelation 13:1–2 is symbolically composed of the precise elements outlined in Daniel 7:4–6 is too coincidental to be dismissed. This symbolic connection between the first three great kings of Daniel and the king of Revelation 13:1-2 suggests the very real possibility that direct connections exist amongst all seven kings related in Revelation 17:10.

If this implied connection does exist between the seven kings of Revelation 17:10, then this would have massive repercussions with respect to the interpretations that could be applied to them. In other words, inherent in the identification of one king is an implied connection that exists among all of them.

This would mean that no king among the seven can stand alone. If you identify one king, then you must explicitly establish his direct connection or relation to all them.

Notice how Nebuchadnezzar, Cyrus, Alexander, and the Roman Prince are symbolically connected in the lion, bear, and leopard representations, while the three kings represented in Caesar Augustus, Tiberius Caesar, and Domitian are not.

1. Nebuchadnezzar (Lion of Daniel 7:4)
2. Cyrus (Bear of Daniel 7:5)

3. Alexander (Leopard of Daniel 7:6)
4. Caesar Augustus (Scarlet-colored beast "was")
5. Tiberius Caesar (Scarlet-colored beast "was")
6. Domitian (Scarlet-colored beast "is not")
7. Roman Prince (Lion, Bear, Leopard)

While a direct symbolic connection exists between Nebuchadnezzar, Cyrus, Alexander, and the Roman prince, this connection appears at odds with the symbolism that binds Caesar Augustus, Tiberius Caesar, and Domitian.

The question that begs is, how does the symbolic connection that binds Nebuchadnezzar, Cyrus, Alexander, and the Roman prince relate to the symbolism that binds Caesar Augustus, Tiberius Caesar, and Domitian?

It appears as if this might be a very daunting task, until the passage of Revelation 17:11 relates there is a yet future eighth king.

CHAPTER 5:

BEAST 6:

THE SATAN-INCARNATE ROMAN PRINCE (DAY 1260 – 2520 OF 70TH WEEK)

And the beast that was, and is not, even he is the eighth, and is of the seven, and goeth into perdition. (Revelation 17:11)

While Revelation 17:10 outlines how there are seven individual kings, verse 11 indicates that there will also be an eighth king. This eighth king is described as being "of" the seven. While this appears to sound like some sort of odd-sounding riddle, the fact of the matter is we already have described what this eighth king is.

Since the identity of the eighth king can also be deciphered in the context of "the beast that was, and is not," and we have already demonstrated how this beast represents Satan, it follows this eighth king must be Satan.

Eighth King of Revelation 17:11
Satan

On page 42, I established how the common thread that binds Caesar Augustus, Tiberius Caesar, and Domitian is the mystery concerning when Satan "was" and when he "is not" on earth.

Since the eighth king of Revelation 17:11 is Satan, and this eighth king fulfills the "yet is" portion concerning when Satan "was, is not, and yet is" in Revelation 17:8, we can now establish the context in which Caesar Augustus, Tiberius Caesar, and Domitian are related. All of them are directly connected to the prophecies concerning when Satan "was," "is not," and "yet is" on earth.

When Satan "was" on earth from 6 B.C. – 33 A.D.
4th King (Caesar Augustus)
5th King (Tiberius Caesar)

When Satan "is not" on earth from 33 A.D. – Present
6th King (Domitian)

When Satan "yet is" from ? – ?
8th King (Satan)

Now that we have established how Satan is the eighth king, and how he is directly connected to Caesar Augustus, Tiberius Caesar, and Domitian, we must now attempt to establish how Satan might be connected to Nebuchadnezzar, Cyrus, Alexander, and the Roman Prince.

Note that each of these four individual kings (Nebuchadnezzar, Cyrus, Alexander, and the Roman Prince) are represented as beasts that rise up out of the sea.

Beasts that rise up out of the sea
1. Nebuchadnezzar (Beast of Daniel 7:4)
2. Cyrus (Beast of Daniel 7:5)
3. Alexander (Beast of Daniel 7:6)
4. Roman Prince (Revelation 13:1–2)

None of the other kings (Augustus, Tiberius, Domitian, or Satan) are represented as beasts that rise up out of the sea. In fact, only Satan (8th king) is represented as a beast at all.

If we can establish how Satan is connected to any of these four individual kings that rise up out of the sea, perhaps we can unlock the connection that exists between Satan and all seven kings in Revelation 17:10.

SATAN AND THE SEVENTH KING

According to Revelation 17:11, Satan is "of" the seven kings. Since logic dictates that the only king among the seven that the eighth king (Satan) could be "of" is the Roman Antichrist represented in the seventh king, it stands to reason that Satan is "of" this seventh king in a peculiarly unique fashion.

What exactly does this mean? How can Satan be the eighth king and yet "of" the seventh at the same time? While there are no clues as to how this could come to pass in the texts of Revelation 17, there does appear to be a major event highlighted in the text of Revelation 13 that suggests how this Roman Prince becomes intertwined with Satan himself.

THE DEADLY WOUND

The passage outlined in Revelation 13:3 describes how Satan becomes "of" this Roman Prince once his deadly wound is healed.

> And I saw one of his heads as it were wounded to death; and his deadly wound was healed: and all the world wondered after the beast. (Revelation 13:3)

Since the only head among the seven this deadly wound can be inflicted upon is the ten-horned head that represents the seventh king, it follows this deadly wound must be incurred by the seventh king.

This deadly wound describes a literal event whereby the Roman Antichrist will be mortally wounded and yet live to tell about it. No doubt his survival will leave doctors and physicians completely baffled. But to the rest of the world, he will be seen as invincible. And to many Jewish and Christian individuals, not to mention the rest of the world, he will be hailed as Messiah and worshiped.

> And they worshiped the dragon which gave power unto the beast: and they worshiped the beast, saying, Who is like unto the beast? Who is able to make war with him? And there was given unto him a mouth speaking great things and blasphemies; and power was given unto him to continue forty and two months. (Revelation 13:4–5)

These passages offer critical insight into the direct relationship between Satan and the Roman Antichrist. Note in Revelation 13:5 how "power was given unto him to continue forty and two months." This "power to continue forty-two months" stands in contrast to the dominion outlined in Revelation 13:2.

THE TWO POWERS

While the power outlined in Revelation 13:2 describes a dominion or authority to rule via the covenant of Daniel 9:27, the power outlined in Revelation 13:5 describes a power "to continue".

"Power" in Revelation 13:2
Outlines a dominion

"Power" in Revelation 13:5
Outlines an ability "to continue"

This power to govern through the covenant is symbolized in the "crown" given the rider of the white horse in Revelation 6:2.

> And I saw, and behold a white horse: and he that sat on him had a bow; and a crown was given unto him: and he went forth conquering, and to conquer. (Revelation 6:2)

This crown given the rider of the white horse symbolizes dominion. Since Satan is the one who gives the Antichrist his power (Revelation 13:2), it only makes sense that the "crown" given the rider on the white horse was given by Satan as well. The dominion Satan will provide the Roman Antichrist allows him to reign the duration of the seventieth week.

Crown given rider of white horse in Revelation 6:2
Symbolizes the dominion Satan provides the Roman Antichrist to reign throughout the seventieth week

We know the Roman Antichrist will reign for seven years instead of only three and one-half because of the implied distinction that exists between the beast of Revelation 13:1-2 before the deadly wound, and the beast of Revelation 13:3 after the deadly wound is healed.

When John relates the vision of Revelation 13:1–2, the beast has already come. This beast represents the identical king symbolized in the "little horn" of Daniel 7:8, Roman Prince of Daniel 9:27, and rider of the white horse in Revelation 6:2.

However, when the text of Revelation 13:5 relates how a power is given him that allows him "to continue" forty-two months, the beast of Revelation 13:1-2 has now become irreparably altered. Something has dramatically changed. The huge textual shift that occurs in Revelation 13:3, when the beast's deadly wound is healed, indicates that we are dealing with something much more than merely a Roman king.

> And I saw one of his heads as it were wounded to death; and his deadly wound was healed: and all the world wondered after the beast. And they worshiped the dragon which gave power unto the beast: and they worshiped the beast, saying, Who is like unto the beast? Who is able to make war with him? And there was given unto him a mouth speaking great things and blasphemies; and power was given unto him to continue forty and two months.
> (Revelation 13:3–5)

These passages strongly suggest this power "to continue" entails a literal power to continue life. If that is the case, then the unique event that distinguishes the "power" to rule from the "power" to continue is the healing of the deadly wound in Revelation 13:3.

Division between power to rule and power to continue
Marked by healing of deadly wound in Revelation 13:3

While these two powers differ in nature and duration, the source of their power remains the same. Both of these powers uniquely derive from Satan.

THE SUPERNATURAL POWERS OF SATAN

How is it possible Satan has the power to heal a deadly wound and allow a man to continue his life? The answer is found in Revelation 9.

> And the fifth angel sounded, and I saw a star fall from heaven unto the earth: and to him was given the key of the bottomless pit. And he opened the bottomless pit; and there arose a smoke out of the pit, as the smoke of a great furnace; and the sun and the air were darkened by reason of the smoke of the pit. And there came out of the smoke locusts upon the earth: and unto them was given power, as the scorpions of earth have power...And they have a King over them, which is the angel of the bottomless pit, whose name in the Hebrew tongue is Abaddon, but in the Greek tongue hath his name Apollyon. (Revelation 9:1–3, 11)

Revelation 9:11 explains how the locusts of the bottomless pit have a "king" over them. This king is named in both the Hebrew and Greek. Abaddon is the Greek name, while Apollyon is the Hebrew name. Each of these names are ascribed to the angel of the bottomless pit. This angel of the bottomless pit is Satan.

Abaddon or Apollyon
Is Satan

The events outlined in Revelation 9 will be cataclysmic for all who dwell upon the earth. Outside of Christ's death and resurrection, Satan's earthly arrival will be the most apocalyptic event the earth will have ever experienced. The consequences surrounding this event will be felt to a staggering degree by everyone.

And worse yet, the scenario outlined in Revelation 12:1-5 when Satan was accompanied to earth with all his fallen angels between 2 B.C. and 33 A.D., will repeat itself when he returns. These "locusts" in Revelation 9 represent the same fallen angels in Revelation 12.

These locusts will be led by the "fallen star" of Revelation 9:1. This "fallen star" represents Satan after he is kicked out of heaven by Michael and his angels in Revelation 12:7–9.

> And there was war in heaven: Michael and his angels fought against the dragon; and the dragon fought and his angels, And prevailed not; neither was there place found anymore in heaven. And the great dragon was cast out, that old serpent called the Devil, and Satan, which deceiveth the whole world: he was cast out into the earth, and his angels were cast out with him. (Revelation 12:7-9)

When Satan is cast out of heaven in Revelation 12:7–9, Revelation 9 picks up where Revelation 12:9 left off. Unlike Satan's previous earthly manifestation in Revelation 12:1–5, this next earthly manifestation is immediately preceded by Satan descending to the bottomless pit.

> And the fifth angel sounded, and I saw a star fall from heaven unto the earth: and to him was given the key to the bottomless pit: and he opened the bottomless pit; and there arose a smoke out of the pit, as the smoke of a giant furnace; and the sun and the air were darkened by reason of the smoke of the pit. (Revelation 9:1–2)

Before Satan returns to earth, he will be forcibly expelled from heaven and descend into the bottomless pit. Note how he is given a key. Exactly what key is Satan given? In Revelation 1:18, we read where Jesus tells John that He possesses the keys of hell and death:

I am he that liveth, and was dead; and, behold, I am alive forever more, Amen; and have the keys of hell and of death.

Revelation 1:18 states that Christ now possesses the keys of hell and death. But note in Revelation 9:2 how a key "given" Satan will allow him access to the bottomless pit.

And he opened the bottomless pit. (Revelation 9:2)

Could this key given Satan be one of the "keys of hell and death" that Christ possesses in Revelation 1:18? I believe it is. It appears this way because the passages of Revelation 9:1–2 state as much.

Since we know this key of the bottomless pit is one of the two keys that Christ possesses in Revelation 1:18, it follows this key given Satan must be the same key of hell that Christ possesses in Revelation 1:18.

While the text of Revelation 9 states that Satan is given the key of the bottomless pit, it is never stated whether or not Satan is given the key of death (note the singular usage of the word "key" in Revelation 9:1).

While the text of Revelation 9:1 never explicitly states the key of death is given to Satan, it is certainly possible Satan will be given such a power. After all, how else is the deadly wound incurred by the Roman Prince healed in Revelation 13:3?

The extraordinary power that will be given Satan for a very brief time needs to be underscored by the point that God places a limitation on the number of saints the Antichrist will be allowed martyr. This is demonstrated in the texts of Revelation 6:9-11.

And when he had opened the fifth seal, I saw under the altar the souls of them that were slain for the word of God, and for the testimony which they held: and they cried with a loud voice, saying, How long, O Lord, holy and true, dost thou not judge and avenge our blood on them that dwell on the earth? And white robes were given unto every one of them; and it was said unto them, that they should rest for a little season, until their fellowservants also and their brethren, that they should be killed as they were, should be fulfilled. (Revelation 6:9-11)

According to verse 11, there is a fixed number of martyred saints that must be fulfilled before God will begin exacting vengeance upon those who slay the saints. While this fixed number is never explicitly related in Revelation 6, it's likely this number is related in the army of horsemen that slay one-third of mankind after the sixth trumpet is sounded.

And the sixth angel sounded, and I heard a voice from the four horns of the golden altar which is before God, saying to the sixth angel which had the trumpet, Loose the four angels which are bound in the great river Euphrates. And the four angels were loosed, which were prepared for an hour, and a day, and a month, and a year to slay the third part of men. And the number of the army of the horsemen were two hundred thousand thousand: and I heard the number of them. (Revelation 9:13-16)

This army of two-hundred million ("two hundred thousand thousand") horsemen was a number that John "heard". Note how John also "heard" the number of the 144,000 sealed Jewish males in Revelation 7:4. John states in Revelation 7:9 that the number of saints is an amount that "no man could number." The fact that John hears the exact number of "horsemen" in Revelation 9:16 is significant, since the "voice" he heard came from the "four horns of the golden altar which is before God" (Rev. 9:13). If it was the voice of God he heard, then the full number of martyred saints will reach its threshold at two-hundred million.

Full number of martyred saints to be fulfilled in Revelation 6:11
Two hundred million?

It is this army of two-hundred million resurrected martyrs that Joel saw in Joel 2:1-11:

Blow ye the trumpet in Zion, and sound an alarm in my holy mountain: let all the inhabitants of the land tremble: for the day of the LORD cometh, for it is nigh at hand; A day of darkness and of gloominess, a day of clouds and of thick darkness, as the morning spread upon the mountains: a great people and a strong; there hath not been ever the like, neither shall be any more after it, even to the years of many generations. A fire devoureth before them; and behind them a flame burneth: the land is as the garden of Eden before them, and behind them a desolate wilderness; yea, and nothing shall escape them. The appearance of them is as the appearance of horses; and as horsemen, so shall they run. Like the noise of chariots on the tops of mountains shall they leap, like the noise of a flame of fire that devoureth the stubble, as a strong people set in battle array. Before their face the people shall be much pained: all faces shall gather blackness. They shall run like mighty men; they shall climb the wall like men of war; and they shall march every one on his ways, and they shall not break their ranks: Neither shall one thrust another; they shall walk every one in his path: and when they fall upon the sword, they shall not be wounded. They shall run to and fro in the city; they shall run upon the wall, they shall climb up upon the houses; they shall enter in at the windows like a thief. The earth shall quake before them; the heavens shall tremble: the sun and the moon shall be dark, and the stars shall withdraw their shining: And the LORD shall utter his voice before his army: for his camp is very great: for he is strong that executeth his word: for the day of the LORD is great and very terrible; and who can abide it? (Joel 2:1-11)

This army of horsemen is the same two-hundred million horsemen related in Revelation 9:16. After the resurrection of the two witnesses in Revelation 11:12, God has taken back the keys of hell and death from Satan, and He is about to hand them over to His Son Jesus Christ. The return of Jesus Christ at the resurrection/rapture is the third woe detailed in Revelation 9:16-19. Upon His return, he will engage against the earth with his two-hundred million horsemen, and one-third of all mankind will be killed.

THE FOURTH HORSEMAN OF THE APOCALYPSE

> And I looked, and behold a pale horse: and his name that sat on him was Death, and Hell followed with him. And power was given him over the fourth part of the earth, to kill with sword, and with hunger, and with death, and with the beasts of the earth. (Revelation 6:8)

The most striking feature given the fourth horseman of the apocalypse is his "name". This is the only rider among the four that is given a name. The fact that "Death" is his name and "Hell" follows with him is an allusion to the the demonic locusts or fallen angels that follow Satan to earth after he opens the bottomless pit in Revelation 9. If the fourth rider's name is "Death," and Satan is the rider whom they follow, then his name is Abaddon or Apollyon. Does "Hell" follow Abaddon to the earth in Revelation 9? It certainly appears to be the case.

The name Hebrew name Abaddon is translated as "destruction". While the name "destruction" appears different than the name "death," the intent is obviously the same: to annihilate.

The text of 1 Thessalonians 5:1-5 warns us how the day this fourth rider begins to ride should not come upon us as thief.

> But of the times and seasons, brethren, ye have no need that I write unto you. For yourselves know perfectly that the day of the Lord so cometh as a thief in the night. For when they shall say, Peace and safety; then sudden destruction shall come upon them, as travail upon a woman with child; and they shall not escape. But ye, brethren, are not in darkness that that day should overtake you as a thief. Ye are all children of light, and the children of the day: we are not of the night, nor of darkness. (1 Thessalonians 5:1-5)

The context of 1 Thessalonians 5:1-4 relates a very important analogy. The analogy that the Apostle Paul is relating is comparing and contrasting the midpoint of Daniel's Seventieth Week with a time frame known as the Day of the Lord. Now, according to Matthew 24:36, only God the Father knows when this Day of the Lord will begin. Therefore, it is true that no one can know exactly when the Day of the Lord will begin. In both instances, the midpoint of Daniel's 70th Week and the Day of the Lord that begins roughly 2.5 years after it will come upon the world "like a thief". The key difference, however, is that while the Day of the Lord will come "like a thief" to both Christians and non-Christians, the midpoint of the seventieth week will only come like a thief upon non-Christians.

Unlike the Day of the Lord, true Christians will know that when "they" (non-Christians) say "peace and safety". In fact, when the midpoint of the seventieth week arrives the moment the Roman Antichrist's deadly wound healed, Satan (Abaddon, Apollyon, or destruction) will already be upon them (non-Christians). But we (Christians) will not be caught "like a thief," since God has told us through his prophets that the midpoint of the 70th Week arrives roughly 1260 days after the Roman Antichrist rises to power with the covenant in the city of Rome.

Note how the allusion "travail upon a woman with child" is used to describe this time. This is an allusion to the passages outlined in Revelation 12:1-5 that relate Satan's earthly advent between 2 B.C. And 33 A.D. The reason 1 Thessalonians 5 alludes to this historical period is because the second half of Daniel's seventieth week replays the vision related in Revelation 12:1-5. The passages of Revelation 12:6-17 detail how the vision is replayed.

HISTORY REPEATS ITSELF

After the Antichrist's deadly wound is healed and the Satanic indwelling takes place, the same thing that happened in 2 B.C. when Satan stood before Israel to persecute her, will happen again.

Notice how the text of Revelation 12:6 begins with a Christian remnant fleeing to a place prepared by God for 1260 days.

And the woman fled into the wilderness, where she hath a place prepared of God, that they should feed her there a thousand two hundred and threescore days. (Revelation 12:6)

The vast number of years that span the passages of Revelation 12:5 and Revelation 12:6 represent the time between Christ's crucifixion (when Jesus was caught up to God's throne in 33 A.D.) and the final 1260 days of the seventieth week. This vast period of time ("telescoping") that separates the two texts represents the time when Satan is not on earth.

Gap of time between Revelation 12:5 and 12:6
Represents when Satan "is not" on earth

The passages that follow after Revelation 12:6 to the end of the chapter in verse 17 specifically relate the final 1260 days of the 70th Week. And since Revelation 12:1–5 encompasses the years 2 B.C. – 33 A.D. (when Satan "was" on earth), the passages related in Revelation 12:6–17 encompass the final 1260 days of the 70th Week (when Satan "yet is" on earth).

Revelation 12:1–5
When Satan "was" on earth between 2 B.C. – 33 A.D.

Revelation 12:6–17
When Satan "yet is" on earth during final 1260 days of the 70th Week

SATAN FULFILLS REVELATION 17:8

While many passages in Revelation 9 and 12 are completely symbolic, the chronology of events seems fairly easy to relate.

After Satan and all his fallen angels are cast out of the heavens (12:9), Christ gives Satan the key of hell (9:1). Satan then descends to the bottomless pit and unlocks it, allowing he and all his demonic hordes to ascend from the bottomless pit to earth (9:2).

Satan's ascension from the bottomless pit in Revelation 9:2 fulfills a critical prophecy regarding the scarlet-colored beast in Revelation 17:8.

> The beast that thou sawest was, and is not; and shall ascend out of the bottomless pit. (Revelation 17:8)

Although this prophecy occurs in Revelation 17:8, we see the actual fulfillment of this prophecy eight chapters earlier—in Revelation 9:2.

On page 33, I highlighted the two preconditions the scarlet-colored beast must fulfill. While the first precondition concerning his ascent "out of the bottomless pit" is fulfilled in Revelation 9:2, the second precondition is fulfilled when they that dwell on the earth, whose names are not written in the Book of Life, shall wonder when they *behold* Satan.

If the word "behold" is literally translated, then this suggests that every person on earth whose name is not written in the Book of Life will physically witness Satan. How is it possible for people on earth to witness Satan? This relates back to the passage of Revelation 13:3 that outlines the healing of the deadly wound.

> And I saw one of his heads as it were wounded to death; and his deadly wound was healed: *and all the world wondered after the beast. And they worshiped the beast*, saying, Who is like unto the beast? Who is able to make war with him? And there was given unto him a mouth speaking great things and blasphemies; and power was given unto him *to continue forty and two months*. And he opened his mouth in blasphemy against God, to blaspheme his name, and his tabernacle, and them that dwell in heaven. And it was given unto him to make war with the saints, and to overcome them: *and power was given him over all kindreds, and tongues, and nations. And all that dwell upon the earth shall worship him, whose names are not*

written in the book of life of the Lamb slain from the foundation of the world. (Revelation 13:3–9) [italics mine]

Note how the passage immediately following Revelation 13:3 relates that "all the world wondered after the beast." The question regarding who "all the world" represents is answered in Revelation 13:8 as all those that "dwell upon the earth...whose names are not written in the Book of Life of the Lamb slain from the foundation of the world."

Once again, note the time in which "all the world wondered" immediately follows the passage relating the healing of the deadly wound. The healing of the deadly wound in Revelation 13:3 marks a huge textual shift, as those whose names are not written in the Book of Life will literally look upon the miraculously healed Antichrist and "wonder". What they will "wonder" is, who exactly is this man? Only they won't this individual king is now Satan himself.

Prophecy of Satan's Return in Revelation 17:8:
1. Shall ascend out of bottomless pit (fulfilled in Revelation 9:2)
2. They that dwell on earth whose names are not written in the book of life shall wonder (fulfilled in Revelation 13:3–8)

Satan's return to earth will begin the final 1260 days of the Roman Antichrist's life. These final 1260 days will begin the precise moment Satan heals him of the deadly wound. This also marks the precise midpoint of Daniel's 70th Week.

The "short space" related in Revelation 17:1 corresponds to the forty-two months outlined in Revelation 13:5.

"Short space" eighth king will continue:
Corresponds to the forty-two months seventh king will continue

The moment the deadly wound incurred by the Roman Prince is "healed," Satan incarnates the body. As a result of this healing, Satan and the Roman Prince become one and the same. During the final

1260 days of the seventieth week, there is no distinction between Satan and the Roman Prince.

Final 1260 days of 70th Week
Satan and the Roman Prince are the same

Ultimately, this means the shift that occurs in Revelation 13:3, when the deadly wound is healed, relates directly to Satan. Therefore, since we know the scarlet-colored beast in Revelation 17 is Satan, the passages that begin in Revelation 13:3 and continue on through Revelation 13:18 are not only pertinent to the Roman Antichrist, but to Satan as well.

Revelation 13:3–18
Relate to Satan-incarnate Antichrist outlined in Revelation 17

It should also be noted here that, according to Revelation 11:7, this Satan-incarnate Roman Prince is directly responsible for the murder of the two witnesses in Revelation 11.

> And when they shall have finished their testimony, *the beast that ascendeth out of the bottomless pit* shall make war with them, and shall overcome them, and kill them.
> (Revelation 11:7) [italics mine]

The beast implicated in the murder of the two witnesses in Revelation 11 is specifically described as "the beast that ascendeth from the bottomless pit."

Since we know this particular beast represents Satan, it follows the two witnesses (who prophesy for exactly 1260 days [Revelation 11:3]) are not killed until sometime after the midpoint of the seventieth week.

Murder of two witnesses in Revelation 11
Must occur after midpoint of 70th Week since it is the Satan-incarnate Antichrist who kills them

Now that we have demonstrated how Satan fulfills the eighth king of Revelation 17:11, we now have all eight kings in view.

"And there are seven kings: five are fallen:"
1. Nebuchadnezzar
2. Cyrus
3. Alexander
4. Caesar Augustus
5. Tiberius Caesar

"and one is..."
6. Domitian

"and the other is not yet come..."
7. Roman Prince

"and when he cometh, he must continue a short space..."
8. Satan (after incarnating the Roman Prince)

OPENING OF FOURTH SEAL CORRESPONDS TO THE SOUNDING OF FIFTH TRUMPET

When cross-referencing the text of Revelation 6:8 with Revelation 9:1, it is extremely important to recognize these two events correspond to one another.

While the opening of the fourth seal marks the midpoint of Daniel's Seventieth Week, when Satan arrives to earth with his demonic multitudes, the sounding of the fifth trumpet marks his ascent from the bottomless pit (with all his demonic "locusts").

Opening of Fourth Seal and Sounding of Fifth Trumpet
Mark the midpoint of the 70th Week

The fifth trumpet ends when with the first "woe". This woe details how those men "which have not the seal of God in their foreheads" (those with the mark of the beast) will be tormented to the point of death, but "death shall flee from them" (Rev. 9:6).

Meanwhile, as those who have the mark of the beast are tormented, those who have the seal of God in their foreheads (the 144,000 of Rev. 7:3) will not be tormented, but divinely protected in the midst of this five-month long demonic plague.

This demonic plague can only occur after the Satan-incarnate Roman Prince has risen to power. And since this rise to power can only take place at the midpoint of the 70th Week, the five month long locusts plague cannot occur until sometime after the midpoint of the seventieth week.

THE SCARLET COLOR

When the beast of Revelation 13:1–2 rises up out of the sea, this marks the rise to power of the seventh king in Revelation 17:10. Unlike the scarlet-colored beast of Revelation 17, the beast of Revelation 13:1-2 rises out of the sea and possesses no color at all.

But the question that presents itself is, if the beast of Revelation 13:1-2 symbolically possesses no color, then does this mean that it remains without color when its deadly wound is healed in Revelation 13:3?

While many pre-millennial scholars acknowledge the Satanic "indwelling" that takes place after the deadly wound is healed in Revelation 13:3, what they fail to account for are the symbolic repercussions this healing implies. The moment the beast of Revelation 13:1-2 is healed of the deadly wound in Revelation 13:3, the great "red" dragon of Revelation 12 indwells its body, causing it to result in the "scarlet-colored" beast of Revelation 17. In other words, the scarlet-colored beast of Revelation 17 is the result of the great red dragon from Revelation 12 indwelling the body of the beast in Revelation 13:1-2 after the deadly wound is healed.

Moment deadly wound is healed
Beast of Revelation 13:1–2 (Seventh king) + Great Red Dragon (Satan) = Scarlet-Colored Beast of Revelation 17:3 (Eighth King)

While this appears to be a radical notion, it makes perfect sense once you recognize that one of the express purposes of offering these symbolic beasts as living-like creatures in the first place was to demonstrate how they are subject to the same changes and manifestations that all literal living creatures undergo.

Note how the scarlet-colored beast in Revelation 17 can be constructed using the combined "bodily" elements related in the beast of Revelation 13 and Great Red Dragon of Revelation 12.

Scarlet-Colored Beast of Revelation 17 is:
1. Mouth of a "lion" (Beast of Revelation 13:1–2)
2. Feet as a "bear" (Beast of Revelation 13:1–2)
3. Like a "leopard" (Beast of Revelation 13:1–2)
4. "Red" (Great Red Dragon of Revelation 12)

The key symbolic characteristic that differentiates the beast of Revelation 13 from great red dragon in Revelation 12 is the color red.

Note how the text of Isaiah 27:1 relates how the LORD will punish the "dragon that is in the sea" in the "day of the Lord".

> In that day the LORD with his sore and great and strong sword shall punish leviathan the piercing serpent, even leviathan that crooked serpent; and he shall slay the dragon that is in the sea. (Isaiah 27:1)

NAMES OF BLASPHEMY

> So he carried me away in the spirit into the wilderness: and I saw a
> woman sit upon a scarlet-colored beast, full of names of blasphemy,
> having seven heads and ten horns. (Revelation 17:3)

According to Revelation 17:3, the scarlet-colored beast is full of
names of blasphemy. Note how the plural "names of blasphemy" are
contrasted against the singular "name of blasphemy" found in the
seven heads of the beast in Revelation 13:1-2.

On page 65 I related how the "name of blasphemy" found on the seven
heads of the beast in Revelation 13:1-2 symbolizes the literal name of
the Antichrist and the city of Rome. If the literal "name of blasphemy"
found on the seven heads symbolizes the literal name of the Antichrist,
then it is only logical presume the plural form of "names of
blasphemy" found on the scarlet-colored beast symbolize something
distinctive about it.

The fact that there is now more than one name that can be ascribed to
the scarlet-colored beast suggests something unique. Note in
Revelation 9 how the name applied to the fallen star of Revelation 9:1
is given twice in Revelation 9:11.

> And they had a king over them, which is the angel of the bottomless
> pit, whose name in the Hebrew tongue is Abaddon, but in the Greek
> tongue hath his name Apollyon. (Revelation 9:11)

The fact that both of these "names" are applied to Satan is significant
in the light of the fact the seven heads of the scarlet-colored beast
possesses "names of blasphemy" upon it. The fact it possesses "names
of blasphemy" metaphorically relates to the fact that Satan has at least
two names, and that he has possessed the body of a human king with
one name.

Names of blasphemy
Symbolically represents the name of the Antichrist (666) together with the name of Satan (Abaddon or Apollyon)

The symbolic representations that bind all eight kings can now be demonstrated in the body-like qualities of the beasts represented in Daniel and Revelation.

1. Nebuchadnezzar (Lion)
2. Cyrus (Bear)
3. Alexander (Leopard)
4. Caesar Augustus (Great "Red" Dragon "was")
5. Tiberius Caesar (Great "Red" Dragon "was")
6. Domitian (Great "Red" Dragon "is not")
7. Roman prince (Lion+Bear+Leopard)
8. Satan (Great "Red" Dragon "yet is")

If the scarlet-colored beast of Revelation 17 can be understood using the combined symbolic elements that relate the beast of Revelation 13:1-2 and great red dragon of Revelation 12, then presumably all the beasts related in the Bible can be understood through this prism.

CHAPTER REVIEW

In this chapter, we established how the eighth king of Revelation 17:11 is Satan. We also demonstrated how the precise event that marks Satan's earthly arrival occurs the moment the deadly wound is healed in Revelation 13:3. We also deduced how this healing will mark the precise midpoint of the 70th Week.

We then established how the nature of the prophecies concerning when Satan "was, is not, and yet is" are fulfilled in Caesar Augustus, Tiberius Caesar, Domitian, and the Roman Prince. What we have yet to establish is how Satan is directly connected to great kings related in Daniel 7:4-6: Nebuchadnezzar, Cyrus, and Alexander.

Since this connection is the final one to establish among the seven kings of Revelation 17:10, then perhaps it isn't a stretch to presume how this final connection would unlock the mystery of the fourth beast in Daniel 7:7.

If the connection that exists between Caesar Augustus, Tiberius Caesar, Domitian, and the Roman Prince is the fact that all of them either are Roman kings.

Roman Kings of Revelation:
1. **Caesar Augustus**
2. **Tiberius Caesar**
3. **Domitian**
4. **Roman Antichrist**

Then it stands to reason that Satan's connection to these four kings is perfectly represented in the city of Rome.

City of Rome
Is the direct connection Satan has to Caesar Augustus, Tiberius Caesar, Domitian, and the Roman Antichrist

The central question that now presents itself is, how is the Satan-incarnate Roman prince connected to the fourth beast in Daniel 7:7?

Keeping in mind that the final condition to be fulfilled concerning the fourth beast is the "diverse kingdom" requirement outlined on page 70, this fourth beast cannot rise to power until the seven remaining kings who did not enter into covenant with the Antichrist at the beginning of the seventieth week agree to enter into covenant with him. When this occurs, only then can the fourth beast to rise to power.

Are there any passages that relate an agreement among all ten kings to give their kingdom to the Antichrist?

CHAPTER 6:

BEAST 7:

THE FOURTH BEAST OF DANIEL 7 (DAY 1260 – 2520 OF 70TH WEEK)

And the ten horns which thou sawest upon the beast, these shall hate the whore, and shall make her desolate and naked, and shall eat her flesh, and burn her with fire. *For God hath put in their hearts to fulfill his will, and to agree, and give their kingdom unto the beast,* until the words of God shall be fulfilled. (Revelation 17:16–17) [italics mine]

The passages related in 17:16-17 fulfill the final "diverse" kingdom condition outlined on page 70. Note how all ten kings "agree" to give the Satan-incarnate Antichrist of Revelation 17 their kingdom.

Beast of Daniel 7:7
1. Diverse King (fulfilled in Revelation 13:1–2)
2. Diverse Kingdom (fulfilled in Revelation 17:17)

Now that all ten kings have "agreed" to give their kingdom to the Antichrist, the fourth beast of Daniel 7:7 can rise up out of the sea.

The fact that this "diverse" kingdom requirement is related in Revelation 17 is no accident. The reason is because the scarlet-colored beast of Revelation 17 and fourth beast of Daniel 7:7 are relating the exact same entity: the Satan-incarnate Antichrist.

Scarlet-Colored Beast of Revelation 17
Represents the Fourth Beast of Daniel 7:7

One of the primary reasons we know that both of them relate the same beast is because Daniel 7:25 and Revelation 17:10 relate how both beasts will endure for exactly three and one-half years.

> And he shall speak great words against the most High, and shall wear out the saints of the most High, and think to change times and laws: and they shall be given into his hand *until a time and times and the dividing time.* (Daniel 7:25) [italics mine]

> And there are seven kings: five are fallen, and one is, and the other is not yet come; and when he cometh, *he must continue a short space.* (Revelation 17:10) [italics mine]

The "short space" the scarlet-colored "must continue" is related in the text of Revelation 13:5.

> And I saw one of his heads as it were wounded to death; and his deadly wound was healed: and all the world wondered after the beast. And they worshiped the dragon which gave power unto the beast: and they worshiped the beast saying, Who is like unto the beast? Who is able to make war with him? And there was given unto him a mouth speaking great things and blasphemies; *and power was given unto him to continue forty and two months.* (Revelation 13:3-5) [italics mine]

Since both the scarlet-colored beast of Revelation 17 and fourth beast of Daniel 7 endure for three and one-half years, we can now examine the symbolic distinctions that exist between them and begin to apply their meanings.

FOURTH BEAST POSSESSES ONE HEAD

Unlike the seven-headed scarlet-colored beast, the fourth beast only possesses one head.

> Then I would know the truth of the fourth beast, which was diverse from all others, exceeding dreadful, whose teeth were of iron, and his nails of brass; which devoured, break in pieces, and stamped the residue with his feet; *And of the ten horns that were in his head...* (Daniel 7:19-20)

The fact this head possesses ten horns is significant since, on page 54, I established how this ten-horned head specifically represents the seventh king (Roman Antichrist) of Revelation 17:10.

Ten-Horned head on Fourth Beast
Specifically relates to Roman Antichrist

FOURTH BEAST RISES FROM SEA

Unlike the scarlet-colored beast that John witnesses "in the wilderness," the fourth beast that Daniel witnesses rises up from the sea.

> And four great beasts came up from the sea, diverse one from another. (Daniel 7:3)

Therefore, two significant differences that exist between the fourth beast and scarlet-colored beast is that, unlike the scarlet-colored beast, the fourth beast only possesses one head and rises up from the sea.

Unlike the Scarlet-Colored Beast
1. Fourth beast possesses one head
2. Fourth beast rises up from sea

In light of the fact the interpretation for the seven heads of the scarlet-colored beast is offered in Revelation 17:9 is extremely significant.

> And here is the mind which hath wisdom. The seven heads are seven mountains, on which the woman sitteth. (Revelation 17:9)

According to Revelation 17:18, this woman represents a "great city" that reigns over the kings of the earth. The text of Revelation 17:5 tells us this great city has a title.

> And upon her forehead was a name written, MYSTERY, BABYLON THE GREAT, THE MOTHER OF HARLOTS AND ABOMINATIONS OF THE EARTH. (Revelation 17:5)

The title applied to this woman is "Mystery Babylon The Great." Since we are told in Revelation 17:18 that she represents a great city, a question as to exactly what city this woman relates.

Back on page 56, I related how one of the key distinctions between the two beasts that rise up out of the sea in Revelation 13:1-2 and Daniel 7:7 is the differing number of heads, and how this distinction might relate to two distinctive geographical locations these beasts will arise.

The fact that Revelation 17:9 defines these seven heads as seven mountains is significant in that these seven mountains can correspond to the city of Rome. Since the beast of Daniel 7:7 is one-headed, this would suggest that it arises in a city that is distinct from Rome.

One-headed fourth beast of Daniel 7
Relates a rise to power in a city that is not Rome

WHERE IS THE FOURTH BEAST?

The text of Daniel 8:10 relates this how fourth beast "waxed great, even to the host of heaven."

The phrase "waxed great, even to the host of heaven" is an allusion to the Tower of Babel in Genesis 11:4.

> And the whole earth was of one language, and of one speech. And it came to pass, as they journeyed from the east, that they found a plain in the land of Shinar; and they dwelt there. And they said one to another, Go to, let us make brick, and burn them throughly. And they had brick for stone, and slime had they for morter. And they said, Go to, let us build us a city and a tower, *whose top may reach unto heaven*; and let us make us a name, lest we be scattered abroad upon the face of the whole earth. (Genesis 11:1-4) [italics mine]

When Nimrod and his followers journeyed east, they happened upon a plain in the land of Shinar. The land of Shinar is located in modern-day province of Babel, near Al-Hillah, Iraq. It was upon this plain that Nimrod constructed the Tower of Babel. His aim, as stated in verse 4, was to build a city and tower that would reach unto heaven.

Genesis 11:5-9 relates how God ultimately thwarted their efforts by confounding their language and scattering them abroad on the face of the earth. But notice in Daniel 8:10 how the text relates this fourth beast of Daniel 7 will succeed in building the city and its tower. In comparing the two texts, it is prophesying that where Nimrod failed to build a city and tower, the Satan-incarnate Antichrist will briefly succeed.

Of course the question is, where will he build this city and tower? Is there more to this Tower of Babel allusion than meets the eye? Will the Satan-incarnate Antichrist construct the city and tower in the same geographical location as Nimrod?

GEOGRAPHY CONFIRMED IN DANIEL 8

> Therefore the he goat waxed very great: and when he was strong, the great horn was broken; and for it came up four notable ones toward the four winds of heaven. And out of them came forth a little horn, which waxed exceeding great, toward the south, and toward the east, and toward the pleasant land. And it waxed great, even to the host of heaven; and it cast down some of the host and of the stars to the ground, and stamped upon them. (Daniel 8:8–10)

The great horn of Daniel 8:8 is Alexander the Great.

After the great horn is broken, "four notable ones" came up. These four notable horns represent the four generals among whom Alexander's kingdom was divided in 323 B.C. These generals were Cassander, Lysimachus, Seleucus, and Ptolemy.

Four Notable Horns
Alexander's four generals

From out of one of these four horns, the "little horn" of Daniel 8:9 will arise. Daniel 8:10 relates how this king will cast down some of the host of the stars, and stamp upon them. Note how the beast of Daniel 7:7 likewise "stamped" the residue with its feet. Cross-referencing the texts of Daniel 7:7 and 8:9, it is also worth noting that both the fourth beast and the "little horn" are described with similar attributes. Both of them are "exceeding great" and "stamped" upon truth.

The key passage that relates the geographic location of the "little horn" is the opening clause of Daniel 8:9, "And out of one of them." This "little horn" will rise to power inside one of the four geographic regions given to Alexander's four generals after his death in 323 B.C.

"And out of one of them" in Daniel 8:9
Denotes a rise to power inside the kingdom of one of Alexander's four generals

It is important to note that each of these regions occupy a land mass east of Rome. The kingdom in which this little horn of Daniel 8:9 will arise specifically represents Seleucid's kingdom. The reason this kingdom specifically represents Seleucid's is because the text of Daniel 11:36 chronicles his rise to power.

> And the king shall do according to his will; and he shall exalt himself, and magnify himself above every god, and shall speak marvelous things against the God of gods, and shall prosper till the indignation be accomplished: for that that is determined shall be done. (Daniel 11:36)

The fact that this text immediately succeeds the account of Antiochus Epiphanes in Daniel 11:35 is significant since Epiphanes himself was a Seleucid king.

Furthermore, only other kingdom from which the little horn could possibly arise would be Ptolemy's Egyptian kingdom. But since Daniel 11:42-43 prophesies that Egypt will be one of the kingdoms the Antichrist will conquer, this leaves Seleucid's kingdom as the only other option.

The Seleucid dynasty lasted from time of Alexander's death in 323 B.C. until 60 B.C. The land mass of Seleucus's kingdom was the largest among the four given to Alexander's generals. At the height of the Seleucid dynasty, its power stretched from the land of modern day Turkey eastward to the border of India. And yes, the city of Babylon in the land of Shinar is located within its border.

The lands of Western Europe are nowhere in view. In light of the fact the seven-headed beast of Revelation 13:1-2 will rise to power in the city of Rome, we know this one-headed fourth beast in Daniel 7 will not. Therefore, the rise to power of this "little horn" in Daniel 8:9 is relating a particular advent of the Antichrist that is distinct from the one that takes place at the beginning of the 70th Week in Rome.

Little horn of Daniel 8:9 relates:
1. Antichrist rises to power inside Seleucid's kingdom
2. His rise to power is distinct from the one that begins the 70th Week in Rome

According to Daniel 8:25, this king will also stand against Jewish Messiah, Jesus Christ, at Armageddon.

> And through his policy also he shall cause craft to prosper in his hand; and he shall magnify himself in his heart, and by peace shall destroy many: *he shall also stand up against the Prince of princes*; but he shall be broken without hand. (Daniel 8:25) [italics mine]

THE STOUT HORN OF DANIEL 7:20

> I considered the horns, and, *behold*, there came up among them another little horn, before whom there were three of the first horns plucked up by the roots: and, *behold*, in this horn were eyes like the eyes of man, and a mouth speaking great things. (Daniel 7:8) [italics mine]

Note how the word "behold" is utilized twice within the text of Daniel 7:8. The first time it is utilized, the "little horn" of Daniel 7:8 causes three horns to be subdued, while the second time it is utilized the horn is seen with "eyes, a mouth, and speaking great things." Note how the descriptions that follow after the second time it is utilized mirror the text of Revelation 13:5.

> ....behold, in this horn were eyes like the eyes of a man, and a mouth speaking great things. (Daniel 7:8)

> And there was given unto him a mouth speaking great things and blasphemies; and power was given unto him to continue forty and two months. (Revelation 13:5)

Since the passage of Revelation 13:5 specifically relate the Satan-incarnate Antichrist, we know this "mouth" speaking great things specifically refers to the Satan-incarnate Antichrist that rises to power at the midpoint of the 70th Week.

Daniel 7:20 offers additional information concerning this horn whose "eyes were like the eyes of man, and a mouth speaking great things."

> And of the ten horns that were in his head, and of the other which came up, and before whom three fell; *even of that horn that had eyes, and a mouth speaking great things, whose look was more stout than his fellows.* (Daniel 7:20) [italics mine]

If you carefully examine the italicized portion of Daniel 7:20, you will notice in final portion how this horn is described as being "more stout" than his fellows.

Judging from the context, it appears something dramatic has happened to the "little horn" of Daniel 7:8. The "little horn" suddenly becomes "stout". We are also told that it "had eyes, a mouth, and spake very great things." The fact that it is suddenly "stout" and "had eyes, a mouth, and spake very great things" is an allusion to the Satanic indwelling.

Stout horn of Daniel 7:20
Represents the indwelling of Satan

Therefore, the text of Daniel 7:20 relates how the distinction between the little horn of Daniel 7:8 and little horn of Daniel 8:9 is the Satanic indwelling that occurs at the midpoint of the seventieth week.

Stout horn of Daniel 7:20
Specifically represents the little horn of Daniel 8:9

And since the little horn Daniel 8:9 represents the fourth beast of Daniel 7, it could be said the stout horn of Daniel 7:20 also specifically represents the fourth beast of Daniel 7.

Stout horn of Daniel 7:20
Specifically represents fourth beast of Daniel 7

Note how all of the conditions that fulfill the Satan-incarnate Antichrist mark the precise midpoint of the 70th Week.

Midpoint of 70th Week is represented when:
1. Fourth beast rises out of sea
2. Little horn of Daniel 8:9 rises to power
3. Little horn of Daniel 7:8 becomes Stout horn of Daniel 7:20
4. Great Red Dragon of Revelation 12 enters body of Beast in Revelation 13 and becomes the Scarlet- colored beast of Revelation 17:3
5. Roman Antichrist's deadly wound is healed in Revelation 13:3
6. Ten kings agree to give kingdom to Roman Antichrist in Revelation 17:17

CHAPTER REVIEW

In this chapter, I related how the fourth beast of Daniel 7:7 and scarlet-colored beast of Revelation 17:3 are dual representations of the Antichrist's rise to power at the midpoint of the 70th Week, when all ten kings will agree to give him their kingdom.

I also related how this Antichrist's rise to power at the midpoint of the 70th Week is fulfilled in the "little horn" of Daniel 8:9. One of the more unique aspects about Daniel 8:9 is that it relates a rise to power inside a specific geographical region that does not include Rome. And since this "little horn" of Daniel 8:9 is the identical fourth beast of Daniel 7 and scarlet-colored beast of Revelation 17, it stands to reason Daniel 8:9 is specifically relating the rise to power of the Satan-incarnate Antichrist at the midpoint of the 70th Week somewhere outside the city of Rome.

However, if the fourth beast of Daniel 7 and scarlet-colored beast of Revelation 17 represent parallel accounts of the Antichrist, then how can one reconcile this against a seven-headed scarlet-colored beast and a one-headed fourth beast?

CHAPTER 7:

MYSTERY OF THE TWO BEASTS

If the fourth beast that Daniel saw and scarlet-colored beast that John saw represent parallel accounts of the Antichrist at the midpoint of the 70th Week, then why are they presented in two different books using dramatically different imagery?

Perhaps the answer to this question has more to do with whom the visions were related than anything else. Given the fact that John was a Hebrew exile of Rome, while Daniel was an exile of Babylon, it is no coincidence that each of them were provided visions that were specific to the era of their exile. While John's visions were specifically tailored for interpretations regarding kings of Rome, Daniel's visions were tailored for kings of Babylon. However, what's even more interesting is that each of them had a specific mystery that only the other could resolve.

THE MYSTERY OF REVELATION

The mystery that John could never resolve is first seen in Revelation 17:3, when he witnesses a woman sit upon the seven heads of the scarlet-colored beast.

> So he carried me away in the spirit into the wilderness: and I saw a woman sit on a scarlet-colored beast, full of names of blasphemy, having seven heads and ten horns. And the woman was arrayed in

purple and scarlet-color, and decked with gold and precious stones and pearls, having a golden cup in her hand full of abominations and filthiness of her fornication: And upon her forehead was a name written, MYSTERY, BABYLON THE GREAT, THE MOTHER OF HARLOTS AND ABOMINATIONS OF THE EARTH. And I saw a woman drunken with the blood of saints, and with the blood of martyrs of Jesus: and when I saw her, I wondered with great admiration. (Revelation 17:3–6)

According to Revelation 17:18, this woman is "that great city that reigneth over the kings of the earth."

Woman of Revelation 17:3
Represents a great city

If one were to literally apply this interpretation to John's day, this city would clearly represent Rome. However, when the text of Revelation 17:8 relates that the scarlet-colored beast "was, is not, and yet is," this clouds that interpretation somewhat, since the beast that "was" is represented in Satan five chapters back in Revelation 12.

Because this beast who "was" specifically represents Satan between the years 2 B.C. – 33 A.D, this does not necessarily imply the woman of Revelation 17:3 "was" as well. It's important to realize that when John first saw the woman in Revelation 17:3 "sit," the implication is that there was a point in time when this woman was *not* sitting on the beast. Therefore, the possibility exists that this woman was not "sitting" on seven heads of the beast in the intervening years between 2 B.C. – 33 A.D.

Furthermore, this woman is described in Revelation 17:6 as "drunken with the blood of saints, and with the blood of the martyrs of Jesus." If this woman in Revelation 17 *was* sitting on the seven heads of the scarlet-colored beast between 2 B.C. – 33 A.D., then this would suggest the city of Rome was martyring Christians in the years leading up to Christ's crucifixion. If that were the case, then history would record massive numbers of Christians were martyred before Christ's crucifixion. Of course, history bares out that no such persecution took place.

Great City of Revelation did not operate between 2 B.C. - 33 A.D
Since massive Christian martyrdom did not take place

By virtue of the fact the book of Revelation relates there are only two windows of time during which Satan is on earth, and history records that during the first time there was no widespread martyrdom of Christians, the only other window of time this martyrdom can take place is the final 1260 days of the seventieth week.

Therefore, since this martyrdom corresponds to time the woman of Revelation 17:3 sits upon the scarlet-colored beast, we can deduce how the only time frame in which this great city can emerge is at the midpoint of the 70th Week.

Woman sits
Midpoint of the 70th Week

Therefore, the mystery of John specifically relates how a "great city" must emerge at the midpoint of the 70th Week.

Mystery of Revelation
A great city emerges at midpoint of 70th Week

THE MYSTERY OF DANIEL

While the Roman exile John relates mystery concerning a great city, the Babylonian exile Daniel also had a mystery. Daniel's mystery is related within the text of Daniel 7:7.

> After this I saw in the night visions, and behold a fourth beast, dreadful and terrible, and strong exceedingly; and it had great iron teeth: it devoured and brake in pieces, and stamped the residue with

the feet of it: and it was diverse than all the beasts that were before it; and it had ten horns. (Daniel 7:7)

If you examine Daniel 7 carefully, you will notice that nowhere in the chapter is there any description concerning the "body" of this beast. There are scattered parts of the beast mentioned: "iron teeth," "ten horns," a "head," and "nails of brass," but nowhere is a full description of the body given.

What is very interesting, however, is that, according to Daniel 7:11, Daniel witnesses the "body" of this fourth beast as it is destroyed.

> I beheld then because of the voice of the great words which the horn spake: I beheld even till the beast was slain, *and his body destroyed,* and given to the burning flame. (Daniel 7:11) [italics mine]

What exactly was this "body" that Daniel saw destroyed? While Daniel acknowledges witnessing the destruction of this beast's body, the strange thing is he never offers any detail concerning what it is. However, while no bodily description is offered, note how this beast does possesses a "ten-horned head".

> Then I would know the truth of the fourth beast, which was diverse from all others, exceeding dreadful, whose teeth were of iron, and his nails of brass; which devoured, brake in pieces, and stamped the residue with his feet; *and of the ten horns that were in his head, and of the other which came up, before whom three fell."* (Daniel 7:19–20) [italics mine]

On page 54 I relate how the ten-horned head in Revelation exclusively relates the seventh king of Revelation 17:10. Since we know this seventh king is the Roman Prince of Revelation 13:1–2, we can state how this vision concerning a ten-horned head specifically relates to the Antichrist.

Ten-horned head of Fourth Beast
Exclusively relates the Antichrist

Furthermore, the text of Daniel 7:25 specifically relates the duration of the fourth beast.

> And he shall speak great words against the most High, and shall wear out the saints of the most High, and think to change times and laws: and they shall be given into his hand until a time, times and the dividing time. (Daniel 7:25)

According to Daniel 7:25, the duration of this fourth beast will encompass 1260 days. Therefore, since the ten-horned head represents the Antichrist, and this fulfills the "diverse" king requirement outlined in Daniel 7:17, we know the mystery of Daniel specifically concerns the "body" of the beast. Contained within this "body" of the beast is the mystery concerning the "diverse" kingdom outlined in Daniel 7:23–25.

Mystery of Daniel
A kingdom the final 1260 days of the 70ᵗʰ Week

UNVEILING THE MYSTERY

When cross-referencing Revelation 17:3 and Daniel 7:7, you will notice that both mysteries concerning the "city" and the "kingdom" share one common feature: The Antichrist.

Beasts of Revelation 17 and Daniel 7:7
Share the same Antichrist

Since we know the Antichrist that both visions share specifically pertain to the Satan-incarnate Antichrist the final 1260 days of the 70ᵗʰ Week, it's likely the missing bodily elements of the fourth beast are contained within the vision relating the scarlet-colored beast of Revelation 17.

Since we know the "body" of the scarlet-colored beast specifically represents Satan, this would mean that the seven heads the woman (great city) sits upon represent the combined elements of the human

Antichrist outlined in Revelation 13:2 ("like a leopard, feet as a bear, and mouth of a lion"), and the great red dragon outlined in Revelation 12 ("red").

Body of scarlet-colored beast in Revelation 17:3
1. Mouth of a lion (Revelation 13:2)
2. Feet as a bear (Revelation 13:2)
3. Like a leopard (Revelation 13:2)
4. Red (Revelation 12:3)

These particular symbols specifically represent Nebuchadnezzar, Cyrus, Alexander, and Satan.

Mystery of fourth kingdom
1. Nebuchadnezzar (lion)
2. Cyrus (bear)
3. Alexander (leopard)
4. Satan (red)

Note that each of these four kings are among the eight kings represented in Revelation 17:10–11. The question that presents itself is, how do these four kings unlock the mystery of the fourth kingdom in Daniel 7:23?

If the body of the scarlet-colored beast is the same "body" that Daniel saw destroyed in Daniel 7:11, then the mystery that both Daniel and John could not know would be answered when the symbols that relate the body of the Satan-incarnate Antichrist are applied.

Mystery of fourth kingdom
1. Nebuchadnezzar
2. Cyrus
3. Alexander
4. Satan

Or

Mystery of great city
1. Nebuchadnezzar
2. Cyrus
3. Alexander
4. Satan

What do we know about the great kingdoms of Alexander, Cyrus, Nebuchadnezzar, **and** a great city?

History records that each of them established their kingdom in the city of Babylon.

City of Babylon
1. Nebuchadnezzar (established Babylonian Empire in 605 B.C.)
2. Cyrus (established Medo-Persian Empire in 539 B.C.)
3. Alexander (established Greek Empire in 331 B.C.)

The mystery of the fourth kingdom related in Daniel 7:23 and great city related in Revelation 17:3–6 are simultaneously fulfilled in Babylon at the midpoint of the 70th Week, when the Satan-incarnate Antichrist will receive the fourth kingdom.

City of Babylon fulfills:
1. Mystery of fourth kingdom at midpoint of 70th Week
2. Mystery of great city at midpoint of 70th Week

Therefore, the mystery of the fourth kingdom is that Satan will receive it in the city of Babylon at the midpoint of the 70th Week.

Mystery of fourth kingdom:
Satan receives fourth kingdom in the city of Babylon at midpoint of the 70th Week

THE FOURTH KINGDOM

Back on page 21, a question arose regarding the distinction between the kingdom represented in the "legs of iron" and "feet and toes of iron and clay" related in Daniel 2:40–41.

Daniel's interpretation of this image is fairly straight-forward until he interprets the fourth kingdom in Daniel 2:40–41.

> And the fourth kingdom shall be strong as iron: forasmuch as iron breaketh in pieces and subdueth all things: and as iron that breaketh all these, shall it break in pieces and bruise. And whereas thou sawest the feet and toes, part of potters' clay, and part of iron, the kingdom shall be divided; but there shall be in it of the strength of the iron, forasmuch as iron is not mixed with clay. (Daniel 2:40–41)

A question arises as to what this fourth kingdom represents? Does it represent the kingdom represented in the "legs of iron," or does it represent the kingdom of "feet and toes of iron and clay"? The text of Daniel does not highlight exactly what distinguishes the "legs of iron" from the "feet and toes of iron and clay".

Perhaps the reason for this lies in the fact that Daniel was an exile of Babylon. If the fourth kingdom the Antichrist receives is established in the city of Babylon, God made the interpretation purposely vague in order to highlight the unique quality this fourth kingdom will possess.

While Daniel was an exile of Babylon, John was an exile of Rome. The book of Revelation reveals that the unique ("diverse") quality this fourth king and kingdom in Daniel 7:7 will possess is a dominion rooted in Satanic power. Since the book of Revelation reveals this quality in Revelation 17, and John was a Roman exile, perhaps the reason God did not reveal it to Daniel was in order to highlight that its revealing would derive from the author whose exile was the result of the very kingdom that would define it. In other words, the fact that John was an exile of Rome, and the entire book of Revelation reveals the Roman Era, the fourth kingdom must be Roman as well.

According to Revelation 17:9, John witnesses the woman sit on the seven heads of the scarlet-colored beast.

And here is the mind which hath wisdom. The seven heads are seven mountains, on which the woman sitteth. (Revelation 17:9)

The fact that John is the one who witnesses the vision is extremely significant since everything he has related up to this point exclusively details the Roman Empire.

Since we know this scarlet-colored represents the identical beast related in Daniel 7:7, and this fourth beast of Daniel represents both a king and a kingdom at the same time, the fact that the scarlet-colored beast possesses seven heads makes it fairly easy to determine the type of king and kingdom this fourth beast is relating.

While the seven heads of the beast in Revelation 13 exclusively relate to a "diverse" Roman king, the seven heads in the scarlet-colored beast relate to both a "diverse" king *and* a "diverse" kingdom at the same time. Therefore, the fact that it possesses seven heads must relate the fact this king and kingdom are Roman.

Seven mountains in Revelation 17:9
Represent a Roman King and a Roman Kingdom

Therefore, this distinction between the "legs of iron" and "feet and toes of iron and clay" can only be the result of the Satanic dominion of the king and kingdom, and not the kind (Roman) of king and kingdom it relates.

Distinction between kingdom represented in "legs of iron" and "feet and toes of iron and clay"
Is Satanic dominion

And since the kingdom of "feet and toes of iron and clay" chronologically arrives after the "legs of iron," this kingdom of "feet and toes of iron and clay" must specifically represent the Roman Empire the last half of the 70th Week.

Kingdom of "feet and toes of iron and clay"
Represents the Roman Empire during the final 1260 days of the 70th Week

Therefore, when the symbolic "woman" sits on the symbolic seven heads that represent seven mountains in Revelation 17:9, this can only represent the Satan-incarnate Antichrist receiving the Roman Empire in the city of Babylon at the midpoint of the 70th Week.

Kingdom of Feet and Toes of Iron and Clay
Represents Satan-incarnate Antichrist receiving the Roman Empire in Babylon at the midpoint of the 70th Week

CHAPTER 8:

BUILDING THE BEAST

What exactly did Daniel witness when he saw the beast of Daniel 7:7 rise up from the sea? Is it possible to know exactly what Daniel witnessed? I believe that we most certainly can.

In order to view this image, we must first examine the beasts that have already been presented.

Beast 1 of Daniel 7:4 = Nebuchadnezzar (605 B.C. – 539 B.C.)

Beast 2 of Daniel 7:5 = Cyrus (539 B.C. – 529 B.C.)

Beast 3 of Daniel 7:6 = Alexander (336 B.C. – 323 B.C.)

Beast 4 of Revelation 12:1 = Satan (2 B.C. – 33 A.D.)

Beast 5 of Revelation 13:1 = Roman Antichrist (Day 1 of 70th Week – Deadly Wound of Revelation 13:3)

Beast 6 of Revelation 17:3 = Satan-Incarnate Roman prince of Daniel 9:27 (Healing of deadly wound – Day 2520 of 70th Week)

Beast 7 of Daniel 7:7 = Satan-Incarnate Roman prince of Daniel 9:27 (Healing of deadly wound – Day 2520 of 70th Week)

Daniel 7:3 outlines these four beast rise up out of the sea. This "sea" represents a gentile origin.

Sea of Daniel 7:3
Represents gentile origin

The text of Daniel 7:7 begins by Daniel declaring he witnesses this fourth beast in "night visions." These "night visions" relate the final 1260 days of the 70th Week.

Night visions of Daniel 7:7
Represent Final 1260 days of the 70th Week

According to Daniel 7:20, this beast also possesses a ten-horned head. Of course, this ten-horned head directly relates to the Roman Antichrist. Since we know the Roman Antichrist is the same beast outlined in Revelation 13:1–2, it follows the symbolic representations offered in Revelation 13:2 must also apply to the beast of Daniel 7:7.

Body of beast in Revelation 13
Applies to same beast in Daniel 7:7

These symbolic descriptions are related in Revelation 13:2.

> And the beast which I saw was *like unto a leopard*, and his *feet were as the feet of a bear*, and his *mouth as the mouth of a lion*: and the dragon gave him his power, and his seat, and great authority. (Revelation 13:2) [italics mine]

The fourth great beast is "like a leopard", possesses the "feet of a bear", and the "mouth of a lion".

Fourth Beast in Daniel 7:7
1. Like a leopard
2. Feet of a bear
3. Mouth of a lion

The text of Daniel 7:7 also relates this beast is "diverse." The dual application of this "diversity" is related in Daniel 7:17,23. This diversity not only applies to a king, but it applies to a kingdom as well.

The text of Revelation reveals the nature of this "diversity" in Revelation 17:3, where we are introduced to a "scarlet-colored" beast. Since this scarlet-colored beast also represents the great "red" dragon of Revelation 12, we know the "diversity" related in Daniel 7:7 specifically relates to a dominion given by Satan.

According to Revelation 17:11, this eighth king is Satan. Since we know the time that Satan receives the kingdom is concurrent to the moment he indwells the body of the Roman Antichrist, and this is symbolically represented in the colors "red" or "scarlet-colored", it follows the beast of Daniel 7:7 must also be scarlet-colored.

Fourth Beast in Daniel 7:7
1. Like a leopard
2. Feet of a bear
3. Mouth of a lion
4. Scarlet-colored

According to Daniel 7:19, the fourth beast also possesses "great iron teeth" and "nails of brass."

The "iron teeth" foreshadow the connection this fourth beast has to Rome. Since this beast simultaneously represents king and kingdom, we know the "iron teeth" foreshadow how the type of king and kingdom this fourth beast represents are both Roman.

Iron teeth of Daniel 7:7
Foreshadow the Roman King and Roman Kingdom it represents

The "nails of brass" foreshadow the unique connection this beast has to belly and thighs of brass represented in Daniel 2:39. Since the fourth beast receives the Roman Empire inside the geographic region once given to Seleucus (Daniel 8:9), the "nails of brass" specifically represent the city of Babylon.

Nails of Brass represent
Foreshadow city of Babylon

Daniel chapter 7 symbolically relates this fourth beast as:

Fourth Beast according to Daniel 7:
1. Rises out of sea (Gentile)
2. Night Visions (Last half of 70th Week)
3. Ten-Horned Head (Roman Antichrist)
4. Great iron teeth (Roman Empire)
5. Nails of brass (City of Babylon)

The book of Revelation reveals the bodily elements as:

Fourth Beast according to Book of Revelation:
1. Like a leopard (Alexander)
2. Feet as a bear (Cyrus)
3. Mouth like a lion (Nebuchadnezzar)
4. Scarlet-colored (Satan)

In order to preview this fourth beast for ourselves, all we do is combine the elements revealed in the book of Revelation with the ones revealed in Daniel 7.

Fourth Beast according to Daniel and Revelation:
1. Rises out of sea (Gentile)
2. Night visions (Last half of 70th Week)
3. Ten horns (Ten Kings)

4. **Ten-horned head (Antichrist)**
5. **Great iron teeth (Roman)**
6. **Nails of brass (City of Babylon)**
7. **Like a Leopard (Alexander)**
8. **Feet as a Bear (Cyrus)**
9. **Mouth of a Lion (Nebuchadnezzar)**
10. **Scarlet-colored (Satan)**

When each of these elements are combined, this approximates the vision that Daniel witnessed in Daniel 7:7.

SATAN IS THE CONNECTION

Now that we have established what these six beasts represented in Daniel 7:4–7, Revelation 13, and 17 precisely relate, we can now establish how Satan is directly connected to each of them. In chronological order, they are:

Beast 1:
King Nebuchadnezzar (Daniel 7:4)

Just as Nebuchadnezzar established his empire in Babylon, Satan will likewise establish his empire in Babylon.

Beast 2:
Cyrus the Great (Daniel 7:5)

Just as Cyrus established his empire in Babylon, Satan will likewise establish his empire in Babylon.

Beast 3:
Alexander the Great (Daniel 7:6)

Just as Alexander established his empire in Babylon, Satan will likewise establish his empire in Babylon.

Beast 4:
When Satan "was" on earth (Revelation 17:3)

Although represented in the beast of Revelation 17:3, the passages chronicling when Satan was on earth are outlined in Revelation 12:1–5. The beginning of this time is marked when Satan provokes Caesar Augustus to tax the world just before Christ's birth in Luke 2:1. Satan does this in order to gather all those from the tribe of David to Bethlehem, making it easier for him to locate and kill Christ as soon as He is born. After Augustus's death in 14 A.D., he was succeeded by Tiberius Caesar. When Christ was crucified in 33 A.D., Satan was literally cast out of the earth. Just as Caesar Augustus and Tiberius Caesar reigned over the Roman Empire, Satan will likewise reign over the Empire.

Beast 5:
Roman Antichrist (Revelation 13:1–2)

Just as the Roman Prince will reign over the Roman Empire, Satan will likewise reign over the Empire.

When the Roman Prince begins to reign over the Empire, he will do so with a covenant. This covenant will mark the beginning of Daniel's Seventieth Week. Three of the ten kings will enter into covenant with him. This covenant will likely be established in Rome.

Beast 6:
Satan-incarnate Antichrist (Revelation 17:3)

Marks Satan's return to earth. Although represented in the beast of Daniel 7:7, the key difference is that John identifies what kingdom (Roman Empire) Satan will reign over. The key passages in the book of Revelation detailing Satan's return to earth are outlined in Revelation 12:6–17, 13:3–18, and 17. This marks the time when Satan will literally incarnate the body of the Antichrist for the final 1260 days of the 70th Week. This will occur the moment the deadly wound is healed in Revelation 13:3. At this point in time all ten kings will agree to give him their kingdom.

This marks the midpoint of the 70th Week and fulfills when Satan will reign over the Roman Empire in Babylon.

Beast 7:
Satan-incarnate Antichrist (Daniel 7:7)

Although the same as Beast 6, the key difference is that Daniel identifies where (city of Babylon) Satan will establish the Roman Empire.

This marks the midpoint of the 70th Week and fulfills when Satan will reign over the Roman Empire in Babylon.

PROPHETIC PATTERNS

The eight kings of Revelation 17:10–11 represent an important pattern that, perhaps, foreshadows the city in which the Antichrist rises to power.

Eight kings of Revelation 17:10–11:
1. Nebuchadnezzar (capital: Babylon)
2. Cyrus (capital: Babylon)
3. Alexander (capital: Babylon)
4. Caesar Augustus (capital: Rome)
5. Tiberius Caesar (capital: Rome)
6. Domitian (capital: Rome)
7. Roman Antichrist (capital: Rome)
8. Satan-incarnate Roman Antichrist (capital: Babylon)

The great image in Daniel 2 also illustrates a pattern. On page 22, I related how the empire skip concerning the Roman Empire ("legs of iron) relates to the foreknowledge of God regarding the New Testament and its cataloging of the Roman Era.

Image of Daniel 2
1. Head of Gold (Old Testament)
2. Chest and Arms of Silver (Old Testament)
3. Belly and Thighs of Brass (Old Testament)
4. Legs of Iron (New Testament)
5. Feet and Toes of Iron and Clay (Old Testament)

Note how this particular pattern finds its parallel in the five beasts that rise up from the sea.

Five Beasts that Rise Up From Sea
1. Beast of Daniel 7:4 (Old Testament)
2. Beast of Daniel 7:5 (Old Testament)
3. Beast of Daniel 7:6 (Old Testament)
4. Beast of Revelation 13:1-2 (New Testament)
5. Beast of Daniel 7:7 (Old Testament)

These five beasts also relate a specific chronology, as evidenced by their animal-like depictions.

Five Beasts that Rise Up From Sea
1. Lion (Daniel 7:4)
2. Bear (Daniel 7:5)
3. Leopard (Daniel 7:6)
4. Lion+Bear+Leopard (Revelation 13:1-2)
5. Lion+Bear+Leopard+Red (Daniel 7:7)

These five beasts ultimately fulfill the Babylon-Rome dynamic that parallel the Old and New Testament.

Five Beasts that Rise Up From of Sea
1. Nebuchadnezzar (capital: Babylon)
2. Cyrus (capital: Babylon)
3. Alexander (capital: Babylon)
4. Roman Antichrist (capital: Rome)
5. Satan-incarnate Roman Antichrist (capital: Babylon)

Image of Daniel 2

1. Head of Gold (Babylonian Empire): 605 – 539 B.C.
(Ended when Cyrus overthrew Belshazzar on Oct. 12, 539 B.C.)

2.Chest and Arms of Silver (Medo-Persian Empire): 539 – 333 B.C.
(Ended when Alexander defeated Darius III in November of 333 B.C. following the Battle at Issus)

3. Belly and Thighs of Brass (Greek Empire): 333 – 30 B.C.
(Ended when Cleopatra died on August 12, 30 B.C. following Battle of Actium)

4. Legs of Iron (Roman Empire) 30 B.C. - Midpoint of 70th Week
(Ends when Ten Kings of Revelation 17:12 give their Roman Kingdom to the Satan-incarnate Antichrist after he is healed of the deadly wound in Revelation 13:3)

5. Feet and Toes of Iron and Clay (Satan's Empire): Midpoint of 70th Week – Armageddon
(Ends when Jesus Christ [Yeshua Ben David] destroys the Satan-incarnate Antichrist in Valley of Jezreel near Mount Megiddo precisely 1260 days after the deadly wound in Revelation 13:3 is healed)

CHAPTER 9:

THE DESTRUCTION OF BABYLON (AFTER MIDPOINT OF 70TH WEEK BUT BEFORE ARMAGEDDON)

In Revelation 17:16–17 a startling prophecy is offered concerning the city of Babylon.

> And the ten horns which thou sawest upon the beast, these shall hate the whore, and shall make her desolate and naked, and shall eat her flesh, and burn her with fire. (Revelation 17:16)

Revelation 17:16 relates how the destruction of Babylon will take place at the hands of the same ten kings who gave the Antichrist their kingdom in Revelation 17:17. While it cannot be argued that the ten kings will execute this destruction, note in the text of Revelation 19:1–2 how it is God Himself who claims responsibility.

> And after these things I heard a great voice of much people in heaven, saying, Alleluia; Salvation, and glory, and honor, and power, unto the Lord Our God: For true and righteous are his judgments: *for he hath judged the great whore*, which did corrupt the earth with her fornication, *and hath avenged the blood of his servants* at her hand. (Revelation 19:1–2) [italics mine]

Judging from the text of Revelation 19:2, it is clear that God is the One ultimately responsible for the destruction of Babylon. One of the primary reasons for this destruction are the prayers of martyred saints in Revelation 6.

When the fifth seal is opened in Revelation 6:10–11, the martyred saints pray for God to exact vengeance for their murders. God tells them to "rest for a little season" until the full number of those killed as they were is fulfilled. The context suggests that there is a set number of martyred Christians that must be fulfilled before God will "avenge" them. It is likely this number of martyred saints specifically relates to the 200,000,000 horsemen described in Revelation 9:16. Whether or not this full number of two-hundred million is fulfilled exclusively within the framework of the 70th Week itself, or is inclusive of all martyrs throughout history is a question that will probably only be answered during the 70th Week.

When the seventh seal is broken in Revelation 8:1, there is silence in heaven for the space of half an hour.

> And when he had opened the seventh seal, there was silence in heaven about the space of half an hour. And I saw the seven angels which stood before God; and to them were given seven trumpets. And another angel came and stood at the altar, having a golden censer; and there was given unto him much incense, that he should offer it with the prayers of all the saints upon the golden altar which was before the throne. *And the smoke of the incense, which came with the prayers of saints, ascended up before God out of the angel's hand. And the angel took the censer, and filled it with fire of the altar, and cast it into the earth: and there were voices, and thunderings, and lightnings, and an earthquake.* (Revelation 8:1–5) [italics mine]

Judging from the context of Revelation 8:4, it appears this "incense" that "ascended up before God" represents the prayers of martyred Christians? Note how the angel takes the censer and casts it toward the earth. Is it possible this censer begins the wrath of God? Moreover, is it possible this censer cast to the earth includes the vengeance God will exact on the city of Babylon?

The "silence in heaven" in heaven for the space of half an hour is a very involved subject that ultimately relates to the general time frame the infamous Resurrection/Rapture of the Church will take place.

While the subject of the Rapture/Resurrection is a fascinating one, it is also a very lengthy one that would require more in-depth discussion that would ultimately derail the point I am trying to make with respect to the timing of the destruction of Babylon. The reason I am citing the text of Revelation 8:1-5 in relation to the destruction of Mystery Babylon is because Revelation 18:21 makes an allusion to the text of Revelation 8:5. If you compare the two texts, you will see what I mean.

> *And a mighty angel took up a stone like a great millstone, and cast it into the sea,* saying, Thus with violence shall that great city Babylon be thrown down, and shall no more be found at all. (Revelation 18:21) [italics mine]

> And another angel came and stood at the altar, having a golden censer; and there was given unto him much incense, that he should offer it with the prayers of all saints upon the golden altar which was before the throne. And the smoke of the incense, which came with the prayers of the saints, ascended up before God out of the angel's hand. *And the angel took the censer, and filled it with the fire of the altar, and cast it into the earth*: and there were voices, and thunderings, and lightnings, and an earthquake. (Revelation 8:3-5) [italics mine]

By virtue of the fact Revelation 19:1-2 describes how it is God Himself who is ultimately responsible for the destruction of Babylon, the text of Revelation 8:5 supports the idea that an "angel" will also have a hand in its destruction.

Are the "mighty angel" of Revelation 18:21 and "angel" of Revelation 8 the same angels? Who is this angel that partakes in the destruction of Mystery Babylon?

Before we begin examining this question, we must first understand the general time frame during the 70th Week the city of Babylon will be destroyed.

TEN KINGS EXECUTE GOD'S WRATH

Revelation 17:14 relates that the same ten kings who destroy Babylon, will also make war with Christ at Armageddon. It is at Armageddon, however, that these ten kings will be killed by Christ Himself.

If the ten kings are overcome by Christ at Armageddon, then it stands to reason the destruction of Babylon by these ten kings must take place before Armageddon.

Destruction of Babylon
Takes place before Armageddon

If the ten kings that destroy Babylon are overcome when Christ destroys them at Armageddon, and the city of Babylon does not emerge as a focal point until the midpoint of the 70th Week, then it stands to reason that its destruction must take place sometime after the midpoint of the 70th Week but before Armageddon.

Destruction of Babylon
Takes place after midpoint but before Armageddon

While it is true the ten kings will destroy Mystery Babylon by fire (Rev. 17:16), note the numerous passages that relate how God Himself is responsible.

> Therefore shall her plagues come in one day, death mourning, and famine; and she shall be utterly burned with fire: for strong is the Lord God who judgeth her. (Revelation 18:8)

> Rejoice over her, thou heaven, and ye holy apostles and prophets; for God hath avenged you on her. (Revelation 18:20)

For true and righteous are his judgments: for he hath judged the great whore, which did corrupt the earth with her fornication, and hath avenged the blood of his servants at her hand. (Revelation 19:2)

After reading these passages, there is little doubt the destruction of Mystery Babylon is the direct result of God's wrath. When God implements His wrath, He will use the ten kings as agents to carry out His wrath against Babylon.

And He will additionally use the mighty angel of Revelation 10.

THE MIGHTY ANGEL OF REVELATION

The mighty angel of Revelation 18:21 that casts the great stone into the sea is the same mighty angel represented in Revelation 10.

And I saw another mighty angel come down from heaven, clothed with a cloud: and a rainbow was upon his head, and his face was as it were the sun, and his feet as pillars of fire: and he had in his hand a little book open: and he set his right foot upon the sea, and his left foot on the earth, And he cried with a loud voice, as when a lion roareth: and when he had cried, seven thunders uttered uttered their voices. And when the seven thunders had uttered their voices, I was about to write: and I heard a voice from heaven saying unto me, Seal up those things which the seven thunders uttered, and write them not. (Revelation 10:1-4)

In verses 5 and 6, we are then told how this angel that stands upon the earth and the sea lifts up his hand to heaven, and swears that there should be time no longer.

This angel that lifts up his hands to heaven is the same man in linen in related in Daniel 12:7. Note how this man, like the mighty angel of Revelation 10, lifts both hands to the heavens.

And I heard the man clothed in linen, which was upon the waters of the river, when he held up his right hand and his left hand unto heaven, and swear by him that liveth forever and ever that it shall be for time, times, and an half; and when he shall have accomplished to scatter the power of the holy people, all these things shall be finished. (Daniel 12:7)

Daniel 12:7 relates how this man in linen is standing upon the waters of the river when he promises a 3.5 year time span until "all these things will be finished."

Is there another biblical account that identifies this man in linen? The answer is, yes. He is identified in Matthew 14:24-27.

But the ship was now in the midst of the sea, tossed with waves: for the wind was contrary. And in the fourth watch of the night Jesus went unto them, walking on the sea. And when the disciples saw him walking on the sea, they were troubled, saying, Be of good cheer; it is I; be not afraid. (Matthew 14:24-27)

The mighty angel of Revelation 10 is the same "man in linen" from Daniel 12:7 that was "upon the water of the rivers". If the "man in linen" who was standing upon the water of the rivers is the same man who walked upon the waters of the Sea of Galilee in Matthew 14 and Mark 6, then the mighty angel of Revelation 10 is Jesus Christ.

Mighty Angel of Revelation 10
Is Jesus Christ

CHAPTER REVIEW

In conclusion, the city of Babylon will play a major role in the final days before Armageddon. The city of Babylon will be directly responsible for an enormous number of martyred Christians, and it will also serve as the epicenter from which the Satan-incarnate Antichrist will reveal himself and establish his final world-wide empire.

Since the destruction of Babylon cannot occur until after it emerges at the midpoint of the 70th Week, and the ten kings that destroy the city are overcome by Christ at Armageddon, it follows this destruction must take place at some point after the midpoint of the 70th Week but before Armageddon.

The destruction of Mystery Babylon occurs as the direct result of God's wrath. Though the ten kings will act as partial agents of God's wrath, there can be no doubt that God Himself is the one completely responsible for its destruction.

In addition to the ten kings, it appears that God will also use a "mighty angel" to exact vengeance upon Babylon. This mighty angel from Revelation 18:21 is likely the same mighty angel seen in Revelation 10. According to Revelation 10, this mighty angel lifts up his hands to heaven as he stands upon the earth and the sea. These passages echo the passage of Daniel 12:7, where a man in linen is seen standing upon the waters of a river. Judging from the text of Matthew 14:24-27, it appears this man in linen that was standing upon the waters of the river is Jesus Christ.

APPENDIX I

THE 7 AND 62 WEEKS TO MESSIAH

THE STARTING CLOCK

And the king [Nebuchadnezzar] spake unto Ashpenaz, the master of eunuchs, that he should bring certain of the children of Israel, and of the king's seed, and of the princes; Children in whom there was no blemish, but well favored, and skillful in all wisdom, and cunning in knowledge, and understanding science, and such as had ability in them to stand in the king's palace, and whom they might teach the tongue of the Chaldeans. (Daniel 1:4–5)

The year is 605 B.C., the year following King Nebuchadnezzar's invasion of Jerusalem. Among the many spoils of Babylon were some of Jerusalem's most gifted children. King Nebuchadnezzar of Babylon sought to teach these children the way of the Babylonians, groom them so that one day they might stand before the king approved in all their ways.

The Hebrew prophet Daniel was one such child. The historical account of Daniel and his Hebrew counterparts Hananiah, Mishael, and Azariah is chronicled in the first part of Daniel. It is written that King Nebuchadnezzar found these four young men ten times better than his own magicians and astrologers in matters of knowledge and understanding:

As for these four children, God gave them knowledge and skill in all learning and wisdom: and Daniel had understanding in all visions and dreams. (Daniel 1:17)

Daniel's particular gift involved the interpretation of visions and dreams. His skill and accuracy in this area was unsurpassed in all Babylon. In fact, during his later years, Daniel foresaw the time when his own people would be released from captivity and granted permission to return to Jerusalem.

In the first year of Darius the son of Ahasuerus, of the seed of the Medes, which was made king over the realm of the Chaldeans. In the first year of his reign I Daniel understood by books the number of the years, whereof the word of the Lord came to Jeremiah the prophet, that he would accomplish seventy years in the desolations of Jerusalem. (Daniel 9:1–2)

Daniel wrote these words in 539 B.C., sixty-seven years into the Babylonian captivity. This particular year marked the first year of the Medo-Persian kingdom in Babylon.

Still in captivity, Daniel began examining the writings of Jeremiah:

> For thus saith the Lord, That after seventy years be accomplished at Babylon I will visit you, and perform my good word toward you, in causing you to return to this place. (Jeremiah 29:10)

Daniel realized that after sixty-seven years of Babylonian captivity, the Hebrew people only had three more years remaining.

Daniel also realized that these seventy years to "be accomplished" had a much larger significance, one that would have a dual prophetic application.

Beginning with the Hebrew exile in 605 B.C., Daniel had received numerous interpretations regarding the strange dreams and visions he encountered. He was fully aware that many of these dreams concerned prophecies that had yet to be fulfilled. The one thing that Daniel was most convicted about was that these dreams encompassed an entire age known today as "The Times of the Gentiles".

Daniel was fully aware the seventy years to be accomplished not only encompassed a literal seventy year Hebrew exile, but corresponded to a literal seventy weeks of years duration that would encompass the entire Gentile Age.

THE LAW OF THE SABBATH

> Speak unto the children of Israel, and say unto them, When ye come into the which I give you, then shall the land keep a sabbath unto the Lord. Six years thou shalt sow thy field and six years thou shalt

prune thy vineyard, and gather in the fruit thereof; But in the seventh year shall be a sabbath of rest unto the land, a sabbath for the Lord: thou shalt neither sow thy field, nor prune thy vineyard. That which growth of its own accord of thy harvest thou shalt not reap, neither gather the grapes of thy vine undressed: for it is a year of rest unto the land. (Leviticus 25:2–5)

In Leviticus 25, God commanded the Hebrews to institute a system of sowing and harvesting the land for six years. On the seventh year they were to do no sowing in order that the soil might replenish itself.

Just as God rested on the seventh day, so to was the land on the seventh year. Designated the "Law of the Sabbath," this law was to be strictly applied once God's people entered into the Holy Land. Note that this law was not only intended to honor God, but it was practical as well. If the soil is not allowed to rest and replenish its nutrients, the soil will die and the land will become barren.

Early Hebrews referred to this seven year cycle in terms of "weeks." Just as we Americans understand one week to encompass seven days, the Hebrews understood one week in terms of seven years.

One Sabbath Week
Is equivalent to seven Hebrew years

And since one Hebrew year is equivalent to 360 days, it follows that one Sabbath week would be the equivalent of 2520 (360x7) days.

Like most Hebrews, Daniel was well aware Sabbath years corresponded to the weeks of years outlined above. Therefore, in reading 2 Chronicles 36:21, it was clear to Daniel that the seventy years determined upon Israel encompassed much more than a seventy year exile.

To fulfill the word of the Lord by the mouth of Jeremiah, until the land had enjoyed her sabbaths: for as long as she lay desolate she kept the sabbath, to fulfill threescore and ten years. (2 Chronicles 36:21)

Since the number of Sabbath years corresponded to the literal number of years of Babylonian exile, Daniel understood these seventy years in terms of Sabbath years.

70 years of Babylonian exile
Would equate to 70 weeks of years

And since the seventy weeks of years encompasses seventy Sabbath years, it would follow that seventy Sabbath years would equate to 490 (70X7) years. Daniel understood that this program of 490 Hebrew years would be used to accomplish the Gentile age.

However, what Daniel did not know, and earnestly sought to know, was the program God would utilize to implement these 490 years.

While diligently seeking to understand this 490 year sequence through prayer and fasting, Daniel 9:25 records that the Angel Gabriel paid him a visit.

> Seventy weeks are determined upon thy people and upon thy holy city, to finish the transgression and to make an end of sins, and to make reconciliation for iniquity, and to bring in everlasting righteousness, and to seal up the vision and prophecy, and to anoint the most Holy. Know therefore and understand that from the going forth of the commandment to restore and build Jerusalem unto the Messiah the Prince shall be seven weeks, and threescore and two weeks: the street shall be built again, and the wall, even in troublous times. (Daniel 9:24–25)

The first thing Gabriel confirms to Daniel is that these seventy weeks of years not only involve the Jewish people, but the holy city of Jerusalem as well. He also learns that once these seventy weeks of years are finished, a time of everlasting righteousness will be manifested.

So how exactly is this program that ushers a time of everlasting righteousness to be implemented? According to Daniel 9:25, this program begins once the commandment to rebuild the city of Jerusalem is brought forth.

JERUSALEM THWARTED

Three years after Gabriel's visit, exactly seventy years into their Babylonian exile, Cyrus the Great of Persia was paid a visit by God. And just as suddenly as King Nebuchadnezzar had overthrown the city of Jerusalem and taken the Hebrews captive, Cyrus the Great released them.

> Now in the first year of Cyrus the king of Persia, that the word of the Lord by mouth of Jeremiah might be fulfilled, the Lord stirred up the spirit of Cyrus king of Persia, that he made a proclamation throughout all his kingdom, and put it also in writing, saying, Thus saith Cyrus king of Persia, the Lord God of heaven hath given me all the kingdoms of the earth; and he hath charged me to build him a house at Jerusalem, which is in Judas. (Ezra 1:1–2)

Quite amazingly, not only were the Jews allowed to return to Jerusalem, but Cyrus had been commissioned by God to financially authorize the assistance they would need to rebuild the city.

Even though many Hebrews (including Daniel) remained behind, most decided to return to Jerusalem.

Ezra 1:7, relates that all of their possessions, including many of the Temple treasures seized by Nebuchadnezzar, were also restored to them. Cyrus had his Treasurer, Mithredath, number them and give them to the newly appointed Judean prince, Sheshbazzar.

However, beginning in Ezra 4, word began to spread among the Samarians that the Hebrews had rebuilt their temple. When this happened, the Samarians asked if they could join the Hebrews in offering Temple sacrifices of their own.

Then they came to Zerubbabel, and to the chief of the fathers, and said unto them, Let us build with you: for we seek your God, as ye do; and we do sacrifice unto him since the days of Esarhaddon king of Assur, which brought us up hither. But Zerubbabel, and to the chief of the fathers of Israel, said unto them, Ye have nothing to do with us to build an house unto our God; but we ourselves together will build unto the Lord God of Israel, as king Cyrus the king of Persia hath commanded us. Then the people of the land weakened the hands of the people of Judas, and troubled them in building, And hired counsellors against them, to frustrate their purpose, all the days of Cyrus king of Persia, even until the reign of Darius king of Persia. (Ezra 4:2–5)

After their request was refused by the Hebrews, the Samarians decided to frustrate their attempts to rebuild Jerusalem. This lasted throughout the tenure of Cyrus the Great's reign, which finally ended with his death in 529 B.C.

When the new Persian king took the throne, the Samarians wasted little time in petitioning him with accusations against Israel.

And in the reign of Ahasuerus, in the beginning of his reign, wrote they unto him an accusation against the inhabitants of Judas and Jerusalem. (Ezra 4:6)

Ahasuerus here is Cambyses, the second Persian king.

Nothing further is said about the grievance Cambyses was delivered or his response to it. However, history records that after his conquest of Egypt in 522 B.C., he unexpectedly died. With no formal heir to the throne in place, civil unrest gripped the mighty Persian Empire.

Some historians record the situation became so tenuous that an impostor king, called Smerdis, took the throne after claiming to be Cambyses's brother. For a brief seven month stretch, this impostor king ruled the Persian Empire.

Recognizing the civil unrest that gripped the Medo-Persian Empire, Samaria quickly seized the opportunity to restate their grievance against Israel to this impostor king.

> Be it known unto the king, that the Jews which came up from thee to us are come unto Jerusalem, building the rebellious and the bad city, and have set up the walls thereof, and joined the foundations. Be it known now unto the king, that, if this city be builded, and the walls set up again, then will they not pay toll, tribute, and custom, and so thou shalt endamage the revenue of the kings. (Ezra 4:12–13)

This new Persian King, who claimed to be the brother of Cambyses and son of Cyrus the Great, was less than eight months into his reign when he was found to be an impostor. The year was 521 B.C., and after his dismissal, Darius I took the throne.

However, for the Hebrews this was too little, too late. The damage had already been done, as Ezra 4:19 relates.

> And I [Smerdis the impostor] commanded, and [a] search hath been made, and it is found that this city [Jerusalem] of old time hath made insurrection against kings, and that rebellion and sedition have been made therein.

When the Samarians received this letter, we read in Ezra 4:23 how they "went up in haste to Jerusalem unto the Jews, and made them cease by force and power." Nearly seventeen years after Cyrus commissioned the city of Jerusalem be rebuilt, the plans were suddenly dashed.

> Then ceased the work of the house of God which is at Jerusalem. So it ceased unto the second year of the reign of Darius king of Persia. (Ezra 4:24)

JERUSALEM REVIVED

Despite the fact Cyrus's edict to rebuild the city was never completed, a remnant of Jews remained in Jerusalem. Over eighty years after Cyrus wrote the edict allowing the city of Jerusalem to be rebuilt, a Hebrew prophet by the name of Nehemiah was in the palace at Shushan—fifty miles east of Babylon—when he heard the disheartening news that Jerusalem had fallen into such a state of disrepair that it was nearly uninhabitable.

This happened in the Jewish month **Chisleau (September-October of the Greek calendars)**.

> And they said to me, The remnant that are left of the captivity there in the province are in great affliction and reproach: the wall of Jerusalem also is broken down, and the gates thereof are burned with fire. And it came to pass when I heard these words, that I sat down and wept, and mourned for certain days, and fasted, and prayed before the God of heaven. (Nehemiah 1:4–5)

Just as Daniel had prayed and fasted in mourning for Jerusalem, Nehemiah fell into mourning as well. His diligent earnestness in fasting and prayer lasted a good six months, when God finally answered him.

Like Daniel, Nehemiah occupied a place of great favor in the king's court. The reigning king at this time was Artaxerxes I. He took the throne in 464 B.C (465 B.C. Julian year), and during the twentieth year of his reign (444 B.C.), he took notice of Nehemiah's sadness.

> And it came to pass in the month Nisan, in the twentieth year of Artaxerxes the king, that wine was before him: and I took up the wine, and gave it unto the king. Now I had not been beforetime sad in his presence. Wherefore the king said unto me, Why is thy countenance sad, seeing thou art not sick? this is nothing but sorrow of heart. Then I was very sore afraid, And said unto the king, Let the king live forever: why should not my countenance be sad, when the city, the place of my fathers' sepulchers, lieth in waste, and the gates

thereof are consumed with fire? Then the king said unto me, For what dost thou make request? So I prayed to the God of heaven. And I said unto the king, If it please the king, and if thy servant have found favor in thy sight, that thou wouldest send me unto Judas, unto the city of my fathers' sepulchers, that I may build it. And the king said unto me, (the queen also sitting by him,) For how long shall that journey be? and when wilt thou return? So it pleased the king to send me; and I set him a time. (Nehemiah 2:1–6)

The important feature of this verse is Nehemiah's sad countenance. Why is Nehemiah sad? Note in the verse above how this particular occasion falls in the month Nisan. This is the first month on the Hebrew calendar. The fact his sad countenance falls on the first month of a new calendar year is not coincidental. Since Nehemiah had been fasting and praying over the city of Jerusalem and its future, this leaves little doubt as to the occasion which caused Nehemiah's sadness: the Hebrew New Year date of 1 Nisan.

Therefore the precise beginning of Daniel's 70 weeks can be located. We find that this date falls on the **first** day of the month **Nisan** during the Hebrew calendar year **3316**.

Using the Gregorian calendar, this date would fall on **March 8, 444 B.C. This date fell on a Thursday.**

GABRIEL'S BROKEN PROPHECY

If thou hadst known, even thou, at least in this thy day, the things which belong unto thy peace! but now they are hid from thine eyes. (Luke 19:42)

Christ uttered these words as he neared the city of Jerusalem on what was supposed to be the most momentous occasion the world had ever seen: the literal disintegration of a Gentile Age, and ushering in of a new, everlasting Messianic Age.

It was to be a time of restoration for the Hebrews. A time marked by unparalleled peace and prosperity.

But it was not be. And as Christ wept (as God did on that day) for His people and His city, it was a day prophesied by the Angel Gabriel over five-hundred years ago.

> Know therefore and understand, that from the going forth of the commandment to restore and to build Jerusalem unto the Messiah the Prince shall be seven weeks, and threescore and two week..
> (Daniel 9:25)

Note how curious it is that Gabriel tells Daniel that from the edict provided Nehemiah in Nehemiah 2:1–6 until Messiah the Prince that **seven weeks and threescore and two weeks** shall elapse. This is a very odd way of expressing sixty-nine weeks, if indeed an unbroken sequence of sixty-nine weeks is what Gabriel was intending to express? Why would Gabriel tell Daniel that seven and threescore and two weeks would elapse when the most efficient way of expressing this would be "nine and threescore weeks"? It strikes me odd the Bible would express this as strangely as it does.

Here is the sequence from the rebuilding of Jerusalem (1 Nisan 3316) to Messiah that Gabriel offers:

From rebuilding of Jerusalem to Messiah
Seven and Sixty-Two Weeks

Note how these two distinct blocks of time are divided at the fiftieth year. It's very interesting to note that this fiftieth year is extremely important when examining Leviticus 25.

> And thou shalt number seven sabbaths [weeks] of years unto thee, seven times seven years; and the space of the seven Sabbaths of years shall be unto thee forty and nine years. Then shalt thou cause the trumpet of the jubilee to sound on the tenth day of the seventh month, in the day of atonement shall ye make the trumpet sound throughout all your land. And ye shall hallow the fiftieth year, and

proclaim liberty throughout all the land unto all the inhabitants thereof; it shall be a jubilee unto you; and ye shall return every man unto his possession, and ye shall return every man unto his family. (Leviticus 25:8–10)

The fiftieth year following seven Sabbath years is proclaimed to be holy. It lasts an entire year, and expressly states that no reaping or sowing is to take place, and that every debt is canceled and every slave set free. This is commonly celebrated as a year of "Jubilee."

50th Year following Seven Sabbaths
Marks the year of Jubilee

Since the fiftieth year is a much hallowed year in terms of Sabbath years, when examining Gabriel's interpretation that Messiah the Prince will appear seven weeks and threescore and two weeks, a question arises as to whether or not the fiftieth year is included in the two sequences.

It doesn't appear the fiftieth year is included in the sequence because of the specific division that distinguishes the two blocks of time.

7 and 62 Weeks
Year of Jubilee is excluded from calculation

Therefore, in examining Daniel 9:25, it's my contention the express number of years when the Messiah was to arrive was not an unbroken string of sixty-nine years, but rather a sequence involving three distinct blocks of time: Seven weeks (49 years), followed by an abbreviated 360 day Jubilee, immediately followed by another unbroken sequence of sixty-two weeks (434 years).

CRUNCHING THE NUMBERS

> On the next day much people that were come to the feast, when they heard that Jesus was coming to Jerusalem, took branches of palm trees, and went forth to meet him, and cried, Hosanna: Blessed is the King of Israel that cometh in the name of the Lord. And Jesus, when he had found a young ass, sat thereon; as it is written. (John 12:12–13)

The feast in the above text refers to the Shabbat HaGadol feast held the Saturday before every Passover.

Since Passover always falls on the 14th day of the month Nisan (Leviticus 23:5), it stands to reason this Saturday before Passover must have fallen on the Saturday before 14 Nisan.

The Passover of 14 Nisan in the year 33 A.D. (3793) fell on Friday April 1st of the Gregorian calendar (April 3rd on the Julian calendar).

Passover of 33 A.D.
Fell on Friday, April 1 (Gregorian date)

The Shabbat HaGadol before the Friday Passover, then must describe the Sabbath of March 26, 33 A.D. (8 Nisan 3793 Hebrew date).

"Feast" of John 12:12
Saturday March 26, 33 A.D. (Gregorian date)

A number of people that were leftover from the Saturday Shabbat had heard that Jesus was coming. When they heard this they went out ("on the next day") to greet him with palm branches, to witness the most historic event the world has ever seen. This was the Messiah's Triumphal Entry, the very day the Angel Gabriel described over 500 years before, precisely 174,240 days from day Nehemiah was commissioned by Artaxerxes I to rebuild the city of Jerusalem. This day fell on Sunday, 9 Nisan 3793.

Messiah's arrival
Sunday 9 Nisan, 3793 (Hebrew date)

Using the Internet calendar converter at www.fourmilab.ch/documents/calendar/ we can break down the calculation like this:

1. "SEVEN WEEKS" (17,640 DAYS)

2. "AND" (360 DAY JUBILEE)

3. "THREE-SCORE AND TWO WEEKS (156,240 DAYS)

OR

"SEVEN WEEKS"
(49 Years or 17,640 days)

Day 1 Begins:
Thursday 1 Nisan 3316 (Hebrew date)

or

March 8, 444 B.C. (Gregorian date)

or

Modified Julian Day -841042

Ends Day 17,640
Wednesday 9 Tammuz 3364 (Hebrew date)

or

June 23, 396 B.C. (Gregorian date)

or

Modified Julian Day -823403

"AND"
(1 Year or 360 Day Jubilee)

Jubilee Begins

Thursday 10 Tammuz 3364 (Hebrew date)

or

June 24, 396 B.C. (Gregorian date)

or

Modified Julian Day -823402

Jubilee Ends

Sunday 15 Tammuz 3365 (Hebrew date)

or

June 19, 395 B.C. (Gregorian date)

or

Modified Julian Day -823042

"THREESCORE AND TWO WEEKS"
(434 Years or 156,240 days)

Begins Day 17,641

Monday 16 Tammuz 3365 (Hebrew date)

or

June 20, 395 B.C. (Gregorian date)

or

Modified Julian Day -823041

Ends Day 173,880

Sunday 9 Nisan 3793 (Hebrew date)

or

March 27, 33 A.D. (Gregorian date)

or

Modified Julian Day -666802

Modified Julian Day is the raw data. Nehemiah was commissioned to rebuild Jerusalem on Modified Julian Day -841042. Christ entered Jerusalem on Palm Sunday of Modified Julian Day -666802. In order to determine the number of days that fell between the two, you just do the math: 841042 – 666802 = 174,240. 174,240 (17,640+360+156,240) days is the precise number of days between Artaxerxes commission in Nehemiah 2 and Jesus Christ's entrance into Jerusalem in Luke 19:41–42.

Proof

Made in the USA